ORTHO'S All About

Creating Japanese Gardens

Written by Alvin Horton

Meredith® Books
Des Moines, Iowa

Ortho® Books
An imprint of Meredith® Books

All About Creating Japanese Gardens
Editor: Marilyn Rogers
Contributing Editor: Michael McCaskey
Contributing Writer: Alvin Horton
Senior Associate Design Director: Tom Wegner
Contributing Designer: Ernie Shelton
Assistant Editor: Harijs Priekulis
Copy Chief: Terri Fredrickson
Copy and Production Editor: Victoria Forlini
Editorial Operations Manager: Karen Schirm
Managers, Book Production: Pam Kvitne,
    Marjorie J. Schenkelberg
Contributing Copy Editors: Barbara Feller-Roth,
    Catherine Hamrick
Contributing Proofreaders: Mary Duerson,
    Kathy Roth Eastman, Elsa Kramer
Contributing Illustrators: Ron Hildebrand, Rick Hanson
Contributing Map Illustrator: Jana Fothergill
Indexer: Ellen Davenport
Electronic Production Coordinator: Paula Forest
Editorial and Design Assistants: Kathleen Stevens,
    Karen McFadden

**Additional Editorial Contributions from
Art Rep Services**
Director: Chip Nadeau
Designers: Ik Design
Illustrator: Rick Hanson

Meredith® Books
Editor in Chief: Linda Raglan Cunningham
Design Director: Matt Strelecki
Executive Editor, Gardening and Home Improvement:
    Benjamin W. Allen
Executive Editor, Gardening: Michael McKinley

Publisher: James D. Blume
Executive Director, Marketing: Jeffrey Myers
Executive Director, New Business Development:
    Todd M. Davis
Executive Director, Sales: Ken Zagor
Director, Operations: George A. Susral
Director, Production: Douglas M. Johnston
Business Director: Jim Leonard

Vice President and General Manager: Douglas J. Guendel

Meredith Publishing Group
President, Publishing Group: Stephen M. Lacy
Vice President-Publishing Director: Bob Mate

Meredith Corporation
Chairman and Chief Executive Officer: William T. Kerr
Chairman of the Executive Committee: E.T. Meredith III

Note to the Readers: Due to differing conditions, tools,
and individual skills, Meredith Corporation assumes no
responsibility for any damages, injuries suffered, or losses
incurred as a result of following the information published
in this book. Before beginning any project, review the
instructions carefully, and if any doubts or questions remain,
consult local experts or authorities. Because codes and
regulations vary greatly, you always should check with
authorities to ensure that your project complies with all
applicable local codes and regulations. Always read and
observe all of the safety precautions provided by
manufacturers of any tools, equipment, or supplies,
and follow all accepted safety procedures.

Thanks to
Janet Anderson

Photographers
(Photographers credited may retain copyright ©
to the listed photographs.)
L = Left, R = Right, C = Center, B = Bottom, T = Top

Karen Bussolini/Positive Images: 60B (Designer: John
McKay, Blois CT); **Patricia J. Bruno:** 25CR; **David
Cavagnaro:** 90B, 99B; **Erica Craddock/Garden Picture
Library:** 50T; **Crandall & Crandall:** 30; **Dianne Dietrich
Leis/Dietrich Photography:** 13, 32T; **Catriona Tudor Erler:**
15C, 16, 25TR, 32B, 71TL, 75RC, 78B, 86C, 87B, 91T,
91C, 98B; **Ron Evans/Garden Picture Library:** 92C;
Derek Fell: 7BR, 14B, 79L, 82T, 105TL; **John Glover:** 7BL,
8BL, 22, 23, 25TL, 29, 36, 43T, 50B, 51T, 58L, 69CT, 69B,
71BR, 85C, 93T, 95B, 97C, 98C, 99T; **John Glover/Garden
Picture Library:** 59; **Anne Gordon Images:** 66TR;
Margaret Hensel/Positive Images: 7CR, 14T; **Marijke
Heuff/Garden Picture Library:** 100; **Jerry Howard/Positive
Images:** 28L, 79R; **Bill Johnson:** 85B; **Wolfgang Kaehler:**
8R, 12, 17, 47B, 54–55, 71TR, 72, 76–77; **Rosemary
Kautzky:** 103C; **Donna & Tom Krischan:** 82B; **Andrew
Lawson:** (6R, 58R, 67CR, 86B, The Julian Dowle
Partnership, RHS Chelsea 1995); 61T, (67T, Designer:
Pamela Woods, Hampton Court 1999), (74, Designer: Terry
Hill, Hampton Court 1999), (75LC, RHS Chelsea 2001),
92T; **Janet Loughrey:** 9BR, 18T, 44B, 51B, 66TL, 68B, 75T,
80, 88T, 96B, 104B; **Allan Mandell:** (9TR, 31L, 40–41, 44T,
67B, Designers: Ilga Jansons & Mike Dryfoos), 15T Daishin-
in, Kyoto, Japan; **Mayer, LeScanff/Garden Picture Library:**
69CR (Pepinieres Plantbessin St. Beuve, France); **Alan
Mitchell/Garden Picture Library:** 102B; **Jerry Pavia:** 60T,
64L, 69TL, 83C, 84B, 87T, 88C, 93C, 96T; **Ben
Phillips/Positive Images:** 98T, 99C; **Michael
Polinder/gardenIMAGE:** 47T; **Richard Shiell:** 62T, 83B,
84C, 86T, 88B, 89B, 94T, 94C, 97T; **Joseph G. Strauch Jr.:**
82C, 83T, 89C; **Ron Sutherland/Garden Picture Library:**
(21, 31R, 64–65, Designer: Professor Fukuhara, Chelsea
Flower Show 2001); 51C; **Michael Thompson:** 6L, 7TL, 9L,
19TR, 24TL, 24B, 25BR, 42, 43B, 52L, 58B, 62BR, 73T,
75BR, 81, 90C, 91B, 95T, 97B, 101, 102T, 103R; **Connie
Toops:** 93B; **Deidra Walpole:** 4, 5, 18BR, 19B, 24TR,
28BR, 33, 37, 61C, 61B, 68T, 71BL, 75BL; **Rick
Wetherbee:** 10, 25BL, 34–35, 89T, 92B; **Justyn Willsmore:**
71C, 84T, 85T, 87C, 90T, 94B; **Steven Wooster/Garden
Picture Library:** 20, 63L

Cover photo: Janet Loughrey (Gardener: Baldassare Mineo)

All of us at Ortho® Books are dedicated to providing you
with the information and ideas you need to enhance your
home and garden. We welcome your comments and
suggestions about this book. Write to us at:
    Meredith Corporation
    Ortho Gardening Books
    1716 Locust St.
    Des Moines, IA 50309–3023

If you would like to purchase any of our gardening, home
improvement, cooking, crafts, or home decorating and
design books, check wherever quality books are sold. Or visit
us at: meredithbooks.com

If you would like more information on other Ortho
products, call 800-225-2883 or visit us at: www.ortho.com

GETTING STARTED

Japanese gardening captures nature's changing moods. In this hill-and-pond garden, a waterfall rushes into a pond that tranquilly mirrors rocks and trees, as koi flash beneath the surface.

The gardening style that evolved in Japan over many centuries is a source of inspiration for gardeners the world over. And for good reason. Though Japanese gardens are not necessarily large and are quite practical, they are tranquil sanctuaries for contemplating nature.

This book is designed to help you conceive, plan, and construct a Japanese-style garden suited to your site and your own needs. You will be introduced to the spirit of the

Ponds or lakes symbolize the sea, just as rocks represent islands. In this setting, water has a calming effect, gently rippling the reflection of a Japanese black pine.

Japanese garden, then led through processes and techniques for planning and building one of your own.

This chapter discusses the garden's relation to nature, a uniquely Japanese concept that has influenced the Japanese garden through its centuries of development, and still does today. The five basic garden styles are described in a historical context. The essential background information supplied in this chapter will prepare you for ideas that come later in the book, and for the challenge of adapting Japanese gardens to the needs of other cultures and regions.

Later chapters examine key design principles and components of the Japanese garden. Step-by-step instructions are presented for choosing and building a garden and for selecting and maintaining plants, including bonsai. Also included are examples of Japanese gardens beautifully suited to their North American context.

Throughout the book, the message of this opening chapter will be kept before you: The Japanese garden is a living embodiment of the natural world, which includes people, too.

JAPANESE GARDENS MIMIC NATURE

In early Japanese history, the garden was no more than an area enclosed by stones, a straw rope, or a fence. The ground inside was sacred; the ground outside, profane. Over time, this garden has been elaborated on, diversified, and refined, but the original concept endures: The Japanese garden remains a place apart, where art and nature collaborate to create serenity. In the ancient Shinto religion, gods are nature spirits, so the Japanese people's perception of the garden as a place to worship nature is not surprising. Whether it is a postage-stamp-size courtyard or balcony, or a spacious stroll garden, in every hour and season the Japanese garden offers the quiet of the natural world.

In Japan, a garden is neither a slice of raw nature enclosed by a wall nor an artificial creation that forces natural materials into unnatural forms to celebrate human ingenuity. Instead, it is a work of art that celebrates nature by capturing its essence. By simplifying, implying, or sometimes symbolizing nature, even a tiny garden can convey the impression of the larger, natural world.

To what in nature does a Japanese garden respond? The answers are various. The garden is a response to space and form within nature: to the landscape itself; the sky above the landscape; the sea around it; and features within it, such as stones, plants, and streams. It is a response to natural time: to the shifts in light during the day, the cycle of seasons with their changing charms, and the enduring aspects of nature. It is also a response to

Through judicious pruning, this Japanese holly (right) is given the character of a windblown sitka spruce clinging to a slope (above).

Sand, rippled by wind (far left), is echoed purposely in pea gravel in Japanese gardens. Raked gravel also represents the waves and ripples of water. The Japanese gardens at the Bloedel Reserve, Bainbridge Island, Washington (above), and Tôfukuji Hojo, Kyoto, Japan (left) are fine examples of this sculpted effect.

people, who as creators and beholders are themselves an essential component of nature.

RESPONSE TO NATURAL SPACE AND FORM

The landscape of Japan is striking, and Japanese gardens reflect this distinctiveness. The coastline, with its numerous islands, huge rock forms, and cliffs rising abruptly from the sea, is dramatically rugged. Wind shapes the trees, creating planes of sparse foliage on widely spaced, sturdy branches. The interior consists largely of steep mountain ranges cloaked with forests and streams and broken by valleys with fields, rivers, and rice paddies. Japanese garden design was historically influenced by the picturesque landscapes of China, and some gardens still reflect that influence. Whether the inspiration is Japanese or foreign, a garden typically suggests a complete, coherent landscape and the subtlest forms, patterns, and unities within it. Successful Japanese gardens are created by practiced, keen observers of nature.

The rounded stones at the base of the boulder (right) simulate the sea washing against natural rock outcroppings found along the Japanese coast (above).

JAPANESE GARDENS MIMIC NATURE
continued

Inspiration for Japanese gardens, such as this one at the Seattle Arboretum (right), comes from natural scenes. The ethereal quality of a leafless tree in winter (below) is an example.

A garden may respond to the passing of time in various ways. The progress of a day is reflected by skilled use of light so that, for example, in the early morning the sun illuminates a group of large, mossy rocks with their nimbus of rock fern. At midday the sun lights a seasonal accent of evergreen clematis flowering atop a fence or a snow-covered lantern nestled among low evergreens. In early afternoon, the sun dapples an earthen wall or a plain of pebbles with the cool, playing shadows of leaves or bare branches.

In the late afternoon, it backlights the perfect form and luminous foliage of an old maple.

The garden often responds to the seasons with short-lived effects that emphasize change and the passage of time. For instance, the intoxicating but brief display of Japanese flowering apricot (*Prunus mume*) blossoms expresses the joy of earliest spring and the renewal of life. Water lilies float languidly on the pond in the heaviest heat of summer. A sprinkling of yellow Chinese redbud leaves on gravel marks the bittersweet melancholy of autumn. Bare stems of the coral bark maple (*Acer palmatum* 'Sango Kaku') gleam in the cold brilliance of winter sunlight and snow, emphasizing icy severity by providing a startling contrast to it.

The subdued, permanent garden features endure through the seasons and over the years, making more poignant the seasonal flashes of color. Rocks and other major landscape forms and the many evergreen plants, with their constant foliage, help to form the garden's backbone and affirm the continuity of life.

PEOPLE IN NATURE

Deeply rooted in Japanese character is the belief that people are a part of nature, not separate from it, and that they need to stay in touch with wild nature in their daily lives.

The rugged beauty of rushing water (right) finds expression in the cascade emptying into the pond (above) and the waterfall that offers a refreshing view from the deck (far right).

Therefore, people have gardens. The proper role of people—in gardens and in nature— is that of participants, not of conquerors and not of observers.

To remind visitors that they are a part of the natural order, artifacts are placed in the garden: a mossy lantern, a sun-bleached water dipper, a worn stepping-stone. Every artifact has a weathered, natural appearance.

To convince visitors to a garden that they are participants, the garden stops short of replicating a landscape. It is left to beholders to complete the picture in their imagination and to experience a simplified landscape as a natural one. When this happens, the garden has succeeded in involving the viewer most intimately—and has become the subject of meditation.

FIVE BASIC GARDEN STYLES:
HILL-AND POND STYLE

In this book the broad label "Japanese garden" covers all styles as though they were one. All have some basic concepts in common, but each style is distinctive.

Although the Japanese recognize a multitude of styles, it is sufficient and most useful for gardeners new to the concept to focus on the five basic garden styles discussed in this chapter. Bear in mind, however, that the separation of "the Japanese garden" into five distinct styles is something of an artificial exercise. Many of the finest Japanese gardens and Japanese-influenced gardens are mixtures

of two or more basic styles. The garden that you plan and build may also be a blending of styles designed to suit your likes and needs.

Common to all the basic styles is a sense of space set apart from the everyday world for communion with nature. In various ways, every Japanese garden suggests the entire natural world. Each style re-creates a paradise where time stands still.

Because each style developed and evolved in a historical context, enough of that context is included here to enhance your understanding and appreciation.

HILL-AND-POND STYLE

Also known as the pond-and-island and the artificial-hill style, this general style

The hill-and-pond style was established more than 2,000 years ago in China. Both literal and symbolic, the style represents coastlines and islands, as well as the structure of the universe as perceived by the ancient Chinese.

HILL-AND-POND STYLE
continued

encompasses a wide range of Japanese gardens. Older than the other types, it originated in China. Like most of the styles, it was available in Japan, as it had been in China, only to nobles and the leisured, rich rulers. The scale of a classic hill-and-pond garden is large, often immense. However, by observing some of the design principles, such as simplification and forced diminishing perspective (see pages 28 and 32), you can create a successful version in a typical urban or suburban yard.

In China around and after 200 B.C., the founder of the Han dynasty and his successors built large gardens whose chief features were artificial lakes or ponds, symbolizing the sea, and hills in the ponds, representing islands. Emperor Wu built a garden in which the islands suggested the Mystic Isles of the Blest,

Stones that seem to float represent the numerous small islands off the coast of Japan. Trees and shrubs represent coastal hills.

Subtle green is preferable to bright green, and evergreen plantings are favored over deciduous ones.

then believed to exist somewhere off the coast of China. The isles, which, according to myth, originally floated, were believed to have been stabilized by the ruler of the universe, who ordered huge sea tortoises to bear them on their backs. But when a giant destroyed many of the tortoises, some islands floated away. The remaining ones, it was thought, could give immortality to whoever found and visited them (and Emperor Wu actually tried). In later Japanese gardens, small garden islands often took forms suggesting tortoises or, less often, the cranes that ferried the immortals to the islands. Both the pine-capped turtle islands and the less representational crane islands, which symbolize long life and good fortune, respectively, remain today as important features of many Japanese gardens.

One elaboration of the hill-and-pond style was the use of vertical rocks and waterfalls to suggest the spectacular mountains in southern China, which were known to the Japanese through Chinese art. Monks and their disciples traveled to the mountains to meditate on the natural splendor. In the hill-and-pond garden, mountains can be an alternative, and sometimes an addition, to islands. The garden became more and more a place for meditation, walled off but containing suggestions of the natural world.

Hill-and-pond gardens, over their long history, have often incorporated whole ranges of mountains, represented by a series of earth mounds, or by low rock forms and low evergreens shaped to suggest the topography of Japan.

Streams are often used instead of, or in addition to, ponds. In hill-and-pond gardens built since Zen Buddhists introduced the concept of the dry-landscape garden in the sixth century, cleverly constructed dry streams, ponds, and waterfalls are used to represent water features.

As with other Japanese garden styles, enduring evergreen plantings predominate over deciduous ones, and green is preferred over over bright colors. Lanterns, trees, streams, bridges, ponds, and other features are in exact proportion to the landscape. The scale of the garden landscape is usually smaller—sometimes remarkably smaller—than that of a comparable landscape in nature. However, it is never so small that stepping-stones, bridges, lanterns, and other functional elements are unusable or out of scale themselves.

Ancient hill-and-pond gardens often covered many acres, but with careful use of the techniques described, even a small backyard can accommodate a hill-and-pond garden.

FIVE BASIC GARDEN STYLES:
DRY-LANDSCAPE STYLE

Karesansui, the dry-landscape or flat-garden style, had precedents early in the evolution of Japanese gardens. It came into its own as a major art form after the advent of Zen Buddhism in the late sixth century and flourished in the small garden spaces of numerous Zen temples and monasteries. Monks used this style as an aid to their contemplation of the essence of nature and human life. The dry-landscape garden is usually viewed from a slightly raised platform or a veranda and is not entered. In many of its forms, it is the most austere, sometimes the most abstract, and today clearly the most modern-looking of Japanese garden styles.

At one of its extremes, this garden is minimalist art, with so little form and detail that the effect is starkly and perhaps obscurely symbolic. Whole landscapes, even the entire natural world, are suggested through a simplification of form and reduction of scale. A typical dry-landscape garden is built in a small, enclosed space that is flat or nearly flat. The sense of enclosure is strong; it consists usually of garden or house walls or a combination of the two. Plant use is minimal, and the few plants used are small and low, spreading or mounding rather than upright. The spare features merely suggest mountains, valleys, plains, and streams or the sea. Water may be represented by an expanse of moss or other fine ground cover such as lawn grass. Typically, however, the dry-landscape garden is made of white sand, fine gravel, stone chips, or pebbles, carefully raked into stylized patterns suggesting the natural patterns of water. An edging of rocks and some plants is common. Simple, naturalistic bridges, such as flat slabs of uncut stone, suit this style. An evergreen backdrop beyond the walls is a standard feature in dry-landscape gardens. Sometimes the designer uses borrowed scenery—a view beyond the garden which appears to be a part of it.

The most celebrated example of this style displays the dry landscape at its most austere

Gravel gardens of Zen Buddhist monasteries are abstracted natural forms intended to encourage contemplation.

Stones suggest islands, and raked gravel represents water in this Japanese dry-landscape style.

Boulders placed on a raised mound represent the Japanese concept of a turtle island. The turtle symbolizes long life.

Mimicking water, a gravel "river" flows beneath a flat-stone bridge.

and abstract. In the garden at the Ryoan-ji monastery in Kyoto, the only plants are mosses on and around the rocks. An area of carefully raked white gravel measuring approximately 30×75 feet surrounds 15 stones arranged in five groups. Beyond the wall, high trees, which did not exist when the garden was built, soften the overall effect. The garden, so startlingly nonrepresentational of familiar landscape, is somehow essentially natural. The arrangement of its stones provides a complex example of asymmetrical balance, a concept defined on page 34.

The other extreme of the dry landscape style, which is relatively naturalistic, is a more recent development and uses the same materials as, and in many ways has much in common with, the more abstract extreme. Seemingly natural water features characterize this style. Streambeds designed to look like actual, dried-up streams are often used. They are built to look so realistic that even viewers who know better might be persuaded that, when the rains come, the streams will flow again. Sometimes these dry streambeds are practical and actually provide drainage for garden runoff.

The dry-landscape style may be adapted to almost any flat garden area, though not in a great expanse: Features of these gardens are designed to be contemplated at fairly close range from one point only. This style is compatible, more than the others, with modern architecture and poses fewer practical problems of creation and maintenance.

Because natural scale can be enormously reduced, the dry-landscape style offers the ideal solution to garden making in a small space. It permits you to represent any natural water feature in your garden when an actual one is not feasible or desirable. A successful dry-landscape garden is also one of the most appealing landscapes in which to contemplate nature and life.

This dry streambed has a practical as well as aesthetic function; it aids runoff during heavy rains. Smooth river stones were placed to look as though they have naturally tumbled down the slope.

FIVE BASIC GARDEN STYLES:
TEA-GARDEN STYLE

The stone path leads to the tea garden, a retreat removed from life's hectic pace.

A 16th-century outgrowth of the Zen influence on Japanese culture, the Japanese tea garden is participatory. It requires that the guest move over a path that leads, in a real as well as a figurative sense, toward a fuller appreciation of natural harmony. This *roji*, or "dewy path," as it is popularly known, has great traditional significance in the tea garden. Along the path the calmness and subtle beauty of the natural world soothe the spirit, remove worldly care, and prepare each guest for the tea ceremony. Meditative detachment from the world and rustic simplicity characterize this style.

The tea garden requires just enough space for a path through a narrow outer garden to an enclosed inner garden, which contains a waiting pavilion, or a bench and a teahouse, and a touch of rock and greenery. The basic layout, which is popular in the United States, lends itself to yards with narrow sides and spacious back areas that can be made private and thus more attractive.

Features of the tea garden are few and simple but must be chosen and arranged with great care. Form follows function perfectly; little about the tea garden is purely ornamental. Stepping-stones, usually surrounded by moss, provide firm, dry footing and mark the path into the inner garden.

The size, surface, and arrangement of the stones can regulate visitors' pace and heighten their awareness of what lies along the way. By slowing the pace, the path can create the illusion of a larger space and a greater distance. A large, comfortable stone can be an invitation to pause and look closely at whatever is placed nearby. The route is softly lit in the evening by simple, weathered stone lanterns. The path is private; its simplicity and seclusion provide a mental and physical transition from the workaday world to the serenity of the teahouse. The mostly evergreen plants are appropriately restrained and unobtrusive, chosen to soothe rather than to excite or startle. Toward the end of the path is a stone water basin surrounded by gravel and perhaps some carefully arranged stones. A stone lantern illuminates the water basin. In an authentic old Japanese tea garden, a nearby well would provide water for the basin and the teahouse.

You can adapt the Japanese tea-garden style, in both form and function, to an occidental setting and lifestyle. In a city or suburb, the tea garden can provide a place of calm for your own solitude and pleasure or for shared enjoyment with a few friends.

Copying every detail of the traditional version is unnecessary. As long as you provide privacy and an atmosphere of intimacy through the use of a roofed structure and fences, walls, or dense evergreen screens, it is possible to achieve the spirit of the Japanese tea garden.

Guests use the rustic water basin to wash their hands and mouths in ritual purification. Instead of being a light source, the stone lantern provides a subtle contrast to natural features.

FIVE BASIC GARDEN STYLES:
STROLL STYLE

Similar in overall appearance, expansiveness, and detail to many hill-and-pond gardens, a stroll garden has, however, a basic functional difference: To be appreciated, it must be walked through and contemplated from many vantage points. Never does it reveal all or even most of itself from any one spot. It provides a quiet haven for meditation, but the viewer must participate more actively than in most gardens of other styles.

Because it must be large enough to accommodate a pathway, the scale of a stroll garden cannot be reduced to fit an

Aptly named, stroll-style gardens are designed to be walked through and viewed from various perspectives. Note how the full length of the path cannot be seen from any one point.

Along an informal gravel trail (below), logs held in place with stakes change levels, forcing strollers to notice the ground, where 'Forest Flame' pieris makes a brilliant accent.

This koi pond is bordered by boulders and a river rock pathway with inset stepping-stones.

their step. Then the stones become smooth, large, and evenly spaced so that at an exactly planned point, strollers will raise their head to see one of the most stunning vistas in the garden.

Paths that repeatedly shift direction by moving in a zigzag pattern rather than along a straight line reveal unexpected vistas and provide fresh views of familiar features that a stroller might already have seen from other angles. In this way, the unique qualities of the stroll garden are revealed.

Stepping-stones leading across the water provide more than an engaging view. They slow down strollers, who naturally want to take sure-footed steps.

The zigzag pattern of the nobedan brings the pleasant surprise of vistas and views seen from a different perspective.

area of only a few square feet, as can a hill-and-pond garden.

A stroll garden must be spacious enough to allow turns in the path and usually some changes in level. A garden of one-third acre or so will provide sufficient area to accommodate a well-designed stroll garden.

The idea of anticipating then discovering beauty detail by detail is central to the stroll-style garden. Such beauty is often subtle, so its discovery requires effort, albeit pleasant, by the stroller.

The design principle of hide and reveal, by which aspects of the garden are sequentially disclosed to the viewer, is especially prominent in stroll gardens. The principle is usually combined with a directing path, a design technique first used in Zen tea gardens.

The design of the stroll garden exercises considerable influence over the strollers. A dramatic example of hide and reveal is found in a garden villa built during Japan's feudal era. Every step along the path is ingeniously planned to control the strollers' experience of the garden. At one point along the path, the stepping-stones become smaller, their surfaces uneven, and their spacing irregular, so that strollers are forced to look down, minding

Stepping-stones end at a classic vignette: a stone lantern, a water bowl, and evergreen plantings.

FIVE BASIC GARDEN STYLES:
COURTYARD STYLE

Courtyard-style Japanese gardens are well suited to contemporary suburban spaces. To avoid reinforcing the minimal size of the space, choose plants that are neither too big nor too small.

Through most of Japanese history, wealth and the ability to make gardens belonged only to the imperial family and the high ranks of nobility. Japanese society was sharply split between upper and lower classes. After the advent of Zen Buddhism, monks were allowed to make small, inexpensive gardens in and around the temples and monasteries, but it was not until the development of a prosperous middle class that gardens became possible for all levels of society. Because some commoners grew richer than their social superiors, it became necessary for them to disguise their affluence. The courtyard style was more private and had wider appeal than the tea garden.

For years before their wide popularity, courtyard gardens had been made at palaces, to be viewed from single rooms or apartments; at monasteries and temples, for peace and meditation; and as the inner portions of tea gardens. In even the humblest and most crowded urban areas, the courtyard style permitted households with a tiny patch of ground to enjoy the living, natural world.

The components of courtyard gardens have varied throughout their history. Following the

invention of tea gardens, courtyard gardens incorporated three traditional basic tea-garden features: a stone lantern, stepping-stones, and a stone water basin. These features, unlike their counterparts in tea gardens, are nearly always ornamental rather than functional, and the courtyard is almost never walked in. Most courtyard gardens use shade tolerant evergreen plants because low light is common to courtyards. Some courtyards use only a stone lantern, a few plants, and moss or gravel; some use plants and a basin; others use only a grouping of plants, such as a simple clump of bamboo. The stark, Zen-inspired gardens (see page 14) use only rocks, gravel, and moss.

The Japanese consider one principle to be of paramount importance in making courtyard gardens: The components must be full-size. Miniaturization would emphasize the smallness of the garden and destroy the illusion of the courtyard's being just one corner of a much larger garden that extends out of view. This illusion is important because a courtyard is usually open only to a patch of sky and therefore can feel more like the indoors than the outdoors. The illusion can be reinforced by the use of tall, pliant plants, such as bamboo, which the least air movement will set into motion. Shadows of the moving plants play across garden surfaces, accentuating the presence of wind and adding to the feeling of the outdoors. An effective courtyard garden might include the trunk of a tree whose top rises above the house, together with smaller plants and realistically scaled artifacts, to create an uncrowded artistic representation of the natural world.

In addition to natural scale, there are other principles essential to making a courtyard garden look its best. Careful maintenance is essential, because untidiness in a closely observed, small space is obvious and unappealing. The absence of water can make the garden appear flat and dull. Frequent

sprinkling of plants, artifacts, and gravel evokes the sweetness and freshness of the outdoors after a rain shower.

The courtyard style offers many possibilities to Americans. Postage-stamp-size patches of land next to a house or in an atrium can be used to simulate the larger landscape. If the garden is located in a small townhouse courtyard, in a minuscule enclosed backyard, or even on a balcony, the living space that looks onto it seems an extension of and not sealed off from the natural world.

Typically, courtyard gardens like this are meant to be viewed from inside by nature-starved residents, rather than used.

DESIGNING
A JAPANESE GARDEN

An appreciation of the spirit of the Japanese garden and an understanding of each of its traditional styles are an essential first step toward creating your own Japanese garden. Resist the impulse to create an instant garden.

Three practical procedures are necessary for the successful building of any garden, whether all or part of an old garden is to be replaced or a new garden created. First, make a careful study of your own needs: What functions will your garden serve? Then study the site closely: What assets and what constraints come with the territory?

Finally—and here the focus narrows specifically to the planning of a Japanese

The elements of a Japanese garden, such as the stone water basin, stepping stones, gravel, and gates, can translate to a Western setting.

garden—determine which principles of Japanese design will serve you best in the plan that you are developing. In this chapter, several basic Japanese design principles are discussed and illustrated.

The first stage of planning, during which you examine your needs and your existing landscape, can be an especially enjoyable and productive game that encourages you to lay aside restraints and dream freely and creatively. Whether you are setting out to design a small entryway garden, a spacious stroll garden, or various gardens around your property, you will profit from this exercise.

Keep a notebook of ideas. You may prefer a garden that is subtly or completely Japanese in style. However, at first it is essential to remain open to all possibilities rather than to confine your thinking to one style.

Include in your notebook existing landscape features, as well as anything that can remind you later of garden designs or features that appeal to you.

This modern garden follows the principles of simplicity, enclosure, and expression of outside landscape within a small space.

A DESIGN CHECKLIST

Spend enough time in the garden site to see what inspirations and feelings it gives you. Think about what the land wants to be. Here the process of determining needs may begin to merge productively with the next step, site analysis. Let the wishing-and-dreaming stage go on for days, weeks, or months until you feel confident that you

Bamboo acts as a sheltering forest of privacy. The drip chain, a practical element, guides rainfall to a sump drain.

Essential to Japanese gardens, bridges bring pleasurable activity, such as viewing the garden and gazing at fish.

A koi pond, with its murmuring, rippling waters, offers instant relaxation while keeping out unpleasant background noise.

have covered all of your garden fantasies and wishes.

Consider each of the following areas and respond to the questions as specifically as possible. Then consider each response and ask yourself questions about it. In the course of this examination, you will begin to analyze your site.

PRIVACY AND OPENNESS: How you respond to these questions may depend on the location of the garden. Consider each question for each of your garden areas.

■ How much, if any, of your garden do you want to be visible from outside your property?

■ If you want public areas, what functions should they serve? Exactly what impressions should they make? What effects should they have on people? What features can you imagine in these private areas?

■ Are any of your needs at odds with the serene spirit of the Japanese garden that was described earlier? If so, how and to what extent? Which conflicts are easily resolvable, and how?

RECREATION: Recreational use means different things to different people.

■ What kinds of outdoor home recreation do you enjoy? What particular features, such as a lawn or a children's play area, does your ideal garden include?

■ Which of these features are high-priority and which are not? List each feature according to its importance.

■ Try to imagine each feature in the context of your Japanese garden. Which recreational features will the garden accommodate and which will require a separate area?

REPOSE: You likely want your garden to be, at least in some part or section, a place of quiet and relaxation.

■ To what extent does your ideal garden offer repose, and what means of repose are most important to you? List priorities and distinguish between essential and optional.

■ What kinds of structures, furnishings, equipment, or other features does each important means of relaxation call for?

■ Because repose is a frame of mind, visualize settings that would best accommodate each

Working with indoor bonsai is a fascinating pastime. Placed in the sunroom, these plants make the garden outside seem larger.

All plants, such as this sedge, Carex comans, need some maintenance. A traditional Japanese garden will require extra care to ensure tidiness.

important means of repose. Write descriptions for each setting, detailing features, structures, and any other elements.

ENTERTAINING: Enjoying your garden in the company of friends may be an important element to consider in your planning.

■ What kinds of entertaining will your ideal garden accommodate? Consider every possibility within your style of living, from sitting and chatting quietly with a few friends to serving (and perhaps cooking) dinner outdoors, to hosting a large cocktail party.

■ Exactly what kinds of facilities and how much room does each type of entertaining require? Keep in mind that you will need room for easy circulation and serving. Will you need lighting for evening entertaining?

■ What arrangement of space and facilities allows large-scale entertaining without eliminating the possibility of intimate, small-scale entertaining or privacy at other times? Do you need separate areas, even separate gardens, for large and small gatherings?

GARDENING AND MAINTENANCE: As important as these considerations are to most homeowners, they are not always given the close attention they demand.

■ Who will build your garden and who will maintain it? Do you want a low-maintenance garden, or are you willing to sustain a higher level of maintenance?

■ Aside from the tending of the Japanese-style ornamental garden, what other kinds of gardening are to be done? For example, does your dream garden contain a lath house, perhaps for bonsai that aren't currently on display in the garden proper? Which kinds of gardening does the main garden accommodate successfully and which require separate areas?

■ Which of your favorite kinds of gardening activities create seasonal messes or unsightliness? Can they be screened from view?

PRACTICAL CONSIDERATIONS: Here are other questions to ask during planning stages.

■ What kinds of work must be done periodically to maintain your garden? What household services, such as garbage removal, require access through your garden space?

■ What kinds of facilities, such as wide and solid pathways, work areas, electrical outlets, lighting, and hose bibs, do your practical needs demand?

■ What kinds of storage areas must claim space that might otherwise be part of your garden? Examples are areas for making compost, collecting refuse, housing heating and air conditioning units, storing garden equipment and tools, potting plants, and holding container plants that are out of bloom or season.

PROBLEMS & SOLUTIONS: *Japanese gardens offer solutions for typical landscape problems.*

Trellis screens are predictable. Using a bamboo hedge instead would soften as well as screen.

Open space calls for enclosure, such as the privacy of a courtyard-style garden.

Air conditioners require visual and auditory camouflage. Consider a bamboo screen and deer scare.

ANALYZING YOUR SITE

There is usually no magic moment when the examination of needs ends and the site analysis begins. Site analysis is a close, methodical look at your property to determine its physical characteristics and horticultural potential, and to weigh your needs list against what the yard will actually allow. Whether you have an undeveloped site or an old garden, only careful analysis can reveal its potential and its limitations.

CHECKING SOIL AND NATURAL ELEMENTS

Having determined through your checklists what you would like from a garden, you are ready to begin matching your needs to the physical realities of your site.

At this stage it is important to work from a base plan: a simple but accurate diagram of your property that includes its dimensions, the placement of the house on the property (with outer doors and windows indicated), and the placement of other buildings, driveways, and paved or constructed features. It is best to use 8×11-inch architect's graph paper, imprinted with a ⅛-inch grid. If your garden area is larger than 30×40 feet, let ⅛ inch represent 1 foot; otherwise, let ¼ inch represent 1 foot. If a map of your property already exists, it's almost certainly drawn to ⅛-inch or ¼-inch scale. You may need to use a tape measure, but if you work from the house plans, a deed map, or a contour map, you can save hours or days of measuring and drawing, especially if you can trace the map. See the sample base plan on page 27.

Unless your property is relatively flat, draw contour lines representing every 1-foot change in level, to show all topographic features and the exact gradient. You can use this information to map drainage patterns: rainwater and irrigation runoff routes and spots where water collects. Bear in mind the practical or legal dangers of channeling your runoff toward your own house or onto neighbors' property.

Now study the natural elements and the soil on your property. The following list includes basic, essential information to be gathered. Record each item on your base map.

MAGNETIC NORTH: Draw an arrow on the map indicating where it is.

WIND DIRECTION: Mark the direction of prevailing winds in your area.

WINDY SPOTS: They are sometimes near corners of the house.

HOT SPOTS: These are the areas that get continuous sunlight.

COLD SPOTS: Because cold air flows downhill, like water, cold spots are usually in the lowest areas, or in areas where flowing air is blocked by walls or fences.

SHADY SPOTS: Bear in mind how shady and sunny spots change with the seasons, with the angle of the sun, and with the leafing and shedding of deciduous trees.

SOIL TYPE AND CONDITION: In some places the native soil is mostly of the same type—for example, all sand or sandy loam or clay. In other areas, or in isolated spots, there can be pockets or veins of heavy, rocky, or very alkaline soil.

CHECKING OTHER NATURAL AND CONSTRUCTED FEATURES

Continue your analysis by studying and noting anything on or within view of the site that might affect its use for a garden. Note and record each on your base map.

EXISTING VEGETATION: Take note especially of mature trees and shrubs, and of such features as areas of bermudagrass or groves of bamboo. Label each.

NATURAL TOPOGRAPHIC FEATURES: If your site has never been bulldozed, and rock outcrops or other natural features remain, consider yourself blessed. They can be special assets in a Japanese garden.

UNATTRACTIVE VIEWS: These include anything from an unattractive house nearby to power poles and wires. Take note of them and think of ways to lessen their impact. Use arrows to indicate unsatisfactory viewpoints, and label each one.

ATTRACTIVE VIEWS: Panoramic views of breathtaking landscapes, a tree or a mass of treetops beyond your property, or a splendid area in an adjoining garden offer possibilities for enlarging the beauty and the scope of your garden. See page 31 for information about borrowed scenery, a technique that allows limited visual assets beyond your site to be "captured." Use arrows to indicate viewpoints from the garden as well as from indoors, and label each.

ESSENTIAL SITE FEATURES: Include on a base plan such features as easements, setbacks, meters, underground and overhead lines, hose bibs, outdoor electrical outlets, downspouts, and drainage systems. Note fences and walls and indicate their height. Indicate the height of each window or glass door above ground level.

Then make a list of your site's problems, in order of severity, and its assets, in order of value or attractiveness. Bearing in mind the spirit of the Japanese garden and remembering your own needs, consider solutions to the problems and uses for the assets.

CHECKING NEEDS AGAINST SITE CHARACTERISTICS

Now the process becomes much more creative and stimulating than simply checking maps for sewer easements and noting elements in the scenery. A plan (or perhaps a range of plans) begins to emerge, as you compare what you want with what you have.

OVERLAYING SKETCHES

At this point lay sheets of tracing paper over your base plan. If the map with all of its site notations becomes cluttered, transfer some notes onto tracing sheets as well.

On the sheets of tracing paper, experiment with various plans for your site. These sketches represent your needs as they are influenced by the limitations and assets of your site. Draw circles (sometimes called balloons) to represent areas and major features. As focal points or areas of the garden emerge, draw dotted arrows to indicate sight lines from viewpoint to object.

Draw large arrows to show circulation patterns. Decide how people will move from one point to another in the garden. Is the route logical and safe? Does it offer the best views of garden features? Include the paths of anyone who routinely or occasionally enters the site.

EVOLVING A PLAN

If your site already has a garden, give careful thought to what, if anything, you will retain. If the old garden still pleases you, and its layout, contours, and atmosphere are suitable, you may decide to make only superficial changes. For instance, you may replace a straight brick path with a curving line of stepping-stones, or a flower bed with a stone arrangement and some evergreens. Or you may cover a brick wall with woven bamboo or greenery.

You may, however, find nothing usable, not even the contouring. Consider carefully before you remove mature trees. Usually you can arrive at a plan that incorporates them.

When you have a basic plan that continues to please you as you review it over a period of time, you are ready to elaborate and refine it by applying the appropriate design principles.

BASE PLAN WITH NOTES

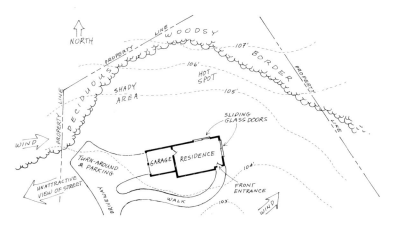

BALLOON SKETCH

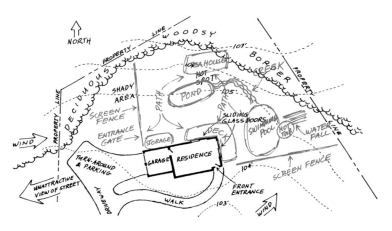

COMPLETED GARDEN DESIGN

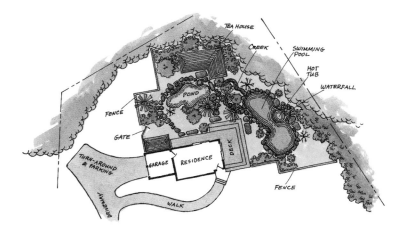

USING JAPANESE DESIGN PRINCIPLES

In Japanese garden design, simplification refers to how a few elements— such as plants, stones, or water features—are carefully placed to intimate the details of nature in a larger sense. The elements may suggest a woodland, a shore, or islands in an ocean.

spirit of a woodland setting. A few well-chosen stones set just so in a bed of raked gravel might produce the impression of a panorama of islands in the ocean. The smallest, simplest courtyard might successfully give the feeling of an expansive garden.

The principle of simplification calls for active participation on the part of the viewer. Following this principle, a skilled garden maker can, with a few simple details, suggest a complex and perhaps expansive scene, and sensitive viewers can then contemplate the scene and fill in the missing elements.

W hat makes a Japanese garden Japanese is more than a sprinkling of the trappings. True, the careful choice and use of garden components, together with an appreciation for the spirit of a Japanese garden and a sound garden plan, are necessary to create a successful Japanese garden. But so are some basic design principles employed for centuries by the Japanese, and sometimes used in other garden styles as well. Discussed here are the key principles of Japanese garden design.

SIMPLIFICATION

The principle of simplification, also known as reductivism or abstraction, is the distillation of nature to its essence. In garden design, this implies reduction in complexity more than in size. The careful selection and arrangement of a few plants, a stream, and several stones might suggest the intricacies and conjure the

Simplicity and unity are achieved in this garden by using only three major plantings.

This rough-hewn lantern exemplifies the simplicity and shape of the boulders that surround it.

Enclosure offers sanctuary. The pavilion and arbor, cloaked by an aged wisteria at peak bloom, frame a lovely scene—the ideal setting for calm.

This phenomenon is rooted in every Eastern religion that recognizes, in any part of nature, intimations of the whole.

ENCLOSURE

Ever since the earliest Japanese gardens were enclosed to separate the sacred ground inside from the profane world outside, the principle of enclosure has been used to set apart the garden sanctuary from the larger world, and to unify the world within the garden. Without the enclosure or implied enclosure, it is very difficult or impossible for the garden or some aspect of it to suggest more than it literally is.

OUTER ENCLOSURE: Beginning on page 76, you will find a discussion of background greenery suitable for enclosing the garden and emphasizing focal points within it, or for suggesting that the garden (particularly an extremely small one) extends farther than it actually does. In very large gardens, masses of trees and constructed or natural hillsides sometimes serve to enclose. Traditional Japanese gardens usually have walls as well, although the massed trees or hillsides may conceal them.

Walls and fences, instead of or in addition to living screens, are the usual means of enclosure in Japanese gardens. The styles, tones, and textures of such enclosures suggest age rather than bright, shiny newness. A weathered wood or bamboo fence or a simple earthen wall provides a discreet enclosure and unites the architecture with the garden.

OVERHEAD ENCLOSURE: A primary purpose of Japanese gardens is to create a place apart, a sanctuary, a setting removed

The fence acts as an enclosure while unifying the garden architecturally. The crabapple screens out the sky's enormity.

from the everyday world. That purpose may be defeated if the garden is as open as a prairie to the sky. This is why one important function of trees in a Japanese (or any) garden is to provide a screen against the sky. A few trees, even one tree in a small garden, diffuse sunlight and create interesting shadows of varying depths. They suggest an enclosing canopy even as they frame sun, moon, stars, and clouds.

The wide eaves that overhang a typical Japanese house do more than allow air circulation during rains. They provide a sense of enclosure. Rather than obliterating the sky and creating a closed atmosphere, trees and eaves create a balance to the openness of the sky. And balance, here as in other aspects of Japanese garden design, is most important.

USING JAPANESE DESIGN PRINCIPLES
continued

THE HOUSE AS ENCLOSURE: Typical Japanese houses have simple exteriors made up of regular, geometric shapes. A certain amount of symmetry is obvious. Their gardens, however, are composed of asymmetrical forms; natural, curving lines are most common. Yet houses and gardens are harmonious.

How is this achieved? Typically a Japanese house provides its occupants and visitors some primary viewpoints into the garden, from both inside and just outside the house. Many courtyard gardens, for example, are created to be viewed only from within the house.

Windows, or entire walls when opened up, remove barriers between the viewer and the garden. Corner posts and other permanent vertical supports frame the views. On some verandas, posts made from unsawed tree trunks suggest actual, living tree trunks, a desirable feature for the foreground. The scope of a view can often be regulated by sliding panels over windows. Floors of houses and verandas are usually raised a foot or so above ground level, affording open views of the garden, whether you are seated or standing. Even tiny courtyard gardens are designed to be seen from raised viewing areas.

Sleeve fences (see page 66), extending from the house, provide effective transitions between building and garden. Verandas, extending over the inner edge of the garden, are also used as transitional devices. Stone- and gravel-filled drip troughs in the ground beneath the eaves combine the architectural lines of the house with the natural stone forms of the garden, just as, architecturally,

Japanese houses are geometric enclosures that coexist with asymmetrical garden forms. Removable walls open the house to nature. Weeping conifers flank the waterfall in this woodland scene.

The view through the gate borrows distant scenery, incorporating it into the garden.

the unsawed posts combine the indoor and outdoor forms. Other transitions may be made by placing container plants just inside the house, or by using split bamboo, rice paper, or some other translucent shades to catch the play of leaf and branch shadows and reflections from water.

Walls or fences that enclose the house and garden further unite both and set them apart from the outer world. Squared-off shrubs, along with rectilinear rocks close to the house and aligned with it, serve to integrate house and garden. Occasionally trees are shaped to echo the pitch and angle of the roof. Gentle slopes with arching eaves mimic the graceful boughs of pines in the garden. Frequently in Japanese gardens, living and architectural forms repeat each other.

BORROWED SCENERY

Shakkei, or, literally, "landscape which is captured alive," is landscape beyond the confines of a garden that has been incorporated into, rather than screened out of, the design. Although enclosure is an important principle, the selective and skillful inclusion of outside landscape can enrich a garden immensely without compromising its sense of seclusion and intimacy. Enclosure isolates, sets a stage, creates a mood. Borrowed scenery provides a balancing (and selective) connection with the world outside, drawing it into the design of the garden, even suggesting in urban gardens, for example, that the garden is in the country. In every style of garden but the tea garden, borrowed scenery is used.

What kind of scenery can be borrowed? Mountains, hills, waterfalls, trees (or just treetops), marshes, lakes, valleys, and the sea

are among natural views traditionally borrowed. Structures of special beauty, simplicity, and antiquity also may be used. Whatever is borrowed should complement the design and intended effects of the garden.

How are objects borrowed? Instead of offering broad, unframed vistas, which can destroy all sense of enclosure, Japanese garden designers skillfully frame a borrowed scene.

A tea garden features a pavilion. The view through its window brings in borrowed scenery, or landscape from beyond.

They use openings, such as windows or passageways in walls, gaps in dense hedges, or low-lying areas in built-up topography, within or just beyond the garden. Traditional devices for framing borrowed scenery include high, branching trees in the foreground or middle ground, which serve to draw the scenery into the design of the garden; a gap or a V in dense groves of trees, designed to frame the desired scenery and screen out the unwanted; and buildings, eaves, and veranda posts that may echo predominant lines of the borrowed scenery and, like the tree trunks, draw the scenery into the composition.

In stroll gardens, viewers following the paths laid for them participate in staged dramas whose object is to present borrowed scenery or features within the garden in the most effective manner.

If your site offers material for borrowed scenery, make sure that whatever you borrow, and the way in which you present it, adds an attractive, harmonious dimension, enhances the feeling of apartness, and maintains the garden's privacy or sense of enclosure.

MANIPULATING PERSPECTIVE AND SCALE

Diminishing perspective is an illusory trick used to make a space seem larger. Strong elements, such as the granite lantern perched on the stone arch and boldly textured shrubs, occupy the foreground. The bridge, with its simple, narrow lines recedes into the background. It also implies there is yet another space to venture to beyond this one.

In designing a Japanese garden, you often will need to prescribe the viewer's sense of distance and scale. You might want to make a large area seem smaller. More likely, you may want to make a small area appear larger, for instance, to trick the viewer into seeing a shallow area as being relatively deep. Similarly, one reason for using the principle of simplification is to suggest a more expansive space than the entire garden, or a section of the garden, actually occupies. Manipulation of perspective is used to create the illusion of depth and distance through practical, mechanistic means.

Forced diminishing perspective is used to give the visual impression of a larger space. It is accomplished by placing large trees, stones, or shrubs in the foreground and small ones in the background. The effect may be created or enhanced by the use of bold textures in the foreground and fine textures in the background; by detail in the foreground and simplicity or lack of detail in the background; by the use of dark or vivid green in the foreground and gray-green or other

Use of large coarse stones in the background and small, fine ones in the foreground makes this space appear smaller.

Coarse-textured plants in front and fine-textured ones behind the water basin make the space seem larger.

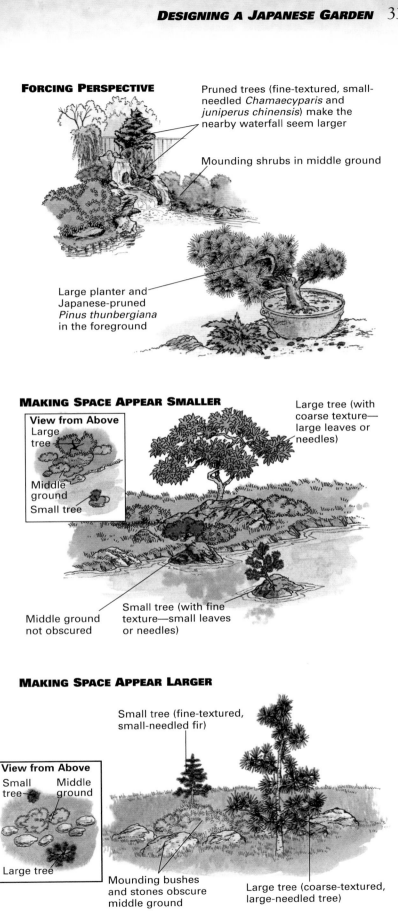

FORCING PERSPECTIVE

Pruned trees (fine-textured, small-needled *Chamaecyparis* and *juniperus chinensis*) make the nearby waterfall seem larger

Mounding shrubs in middle ground

Large planter and Japanese-pruned *Pinus thunbergiana* in the foreground

MAKING SPACE APPEAR SMALLER

View from Above
Large tree

Middle ground

Small tree

Large tree (with coarse texture—large leaves or needles)

Middle ground not obscured

Small tree (with fine texture—small leaves or needles)

MAKING SPACE APPEAR LARGER

Small tree (fine-textured, small-needled fir)

View from Above
Small tree   Middle ground

Large tree

Mounding bushes and stones obscure middle ground

Large tree (coarse-textured, large-needled tree)

soft, muted plant tones in the background, to suggest hazy distances. Similarly, if a path, streambed, or peninsula is tapered so that it narrows at the far end and recedes from the viewing point, it will seem longer than it is.

The effect of forcing perspective is enhanced by another perspective effect called obscuring the middle ground. In Japanese garden design, perspective is divided into three planes: foreground, middle ground, and background. If the middle ground can be partially obscured by low, mounding rocks or plants, the continuous visual link between foreground and background is interrupted, making the background seem disconnected and distant.

A third method of forming perspective and the sense of scale is miniaturization. For example, imagine that near the bank of a pond in a garden lies a partially submerged boat, apparently full-sized. Because nothing nearby gives a sense of scale, this miniature boat does not give the impression of being small, and its presence makes the entire garden scene seem more spacious than it is.

To make an area seem shallower or smaller, all of the techniques mentioned above used in reverse will bring the background visually closer to the foreground. If you have a site whose depth diminishes the sense of enclosure and intimacy you desire, use larger forms, bolder colors and textures, and more details in the background, and make sure that the middle ground is not obscured. Taper pathways and other linear features so that their narrower ends are closer to the viewer.

ASYMMETRICAL BALANCE AND UNITY

The Japanese achieve visual balance in garden design through the use of asymmetrical balance (also called occult balance). Alien to the Japanese is bilateral symmetry, in which the various elements are balanced in even-numbered groups of equivalent size (historically the hallmark of most formal Western design). To make each side of a garden or feature mirror the other is unthinkable. The Japanese use the subtler, more natural asymmetrical balance in stone placement, stroll-path layout, and arrangement of most other garden features and overall garden design.

A seesaw holding two people of identical weight will be symmetrically balanced if both are at an equal distance from the fulcrum in the center. Two people of different weights can also balance the plank if the lighter sits farther away from the fulcrum than the heavier. The difference in distance of the two people from the fulcrum will balance the plank asymmetrically.

In design, visual (not actual) weight must be balanced. A large stone has greater visual weight than a small one, even if the larger is a sponge rock weighing 30 pounds and the smaller a lump of granite weighing 70 pounds.

Psychological impact also influences visual weight. A gilded statue has more psychological weight than a shrub or stone of equal mass standing in the same position. A cluster of red flowers has more visual weight than a cluster of green leaves.

In a Japanese garden, asymmetrically balanced designs usually follow the lines of a scalene triangle, each side of which is a different length. For instance, in a group of stones, the central and tallest stone (or the vertical line that marks its center) represents the fulcrum, or balance point, and is flanked by two other stones of unequal sizes, to form a scalene triangle. Smaller "helping stones" (or mounding, dense plants visually used in a similar way) may be added to enrich and extend the group, but the asymmetrical balance is maintained.

Interlocking scalene triangles (that is, a series of connected scalene triangles) may be used to develop more extensive groupings. Because groupings are three-dimensional, not flat, the different elements are never lined up on a single plane but, instead, are staggered so that they lie at varying distances from the viewer. If the grouping will be seen from more than one viewpoint, the designer is challenged to make an arrangement that is balanced from every angle or, at least, from several angles. Japanese garden design also

A moss-covered stone lantern visually balances the airy golden maple.

ASYMMETRICAL BALANCE AND UNITY
continued

Repetition contributes to unity. Boulders rising from a sea of evergreens are echoed in smaller stones of the same type and shape at the base of the golden bamboo edging.

takes into account the relationship between form and emptiness, an important aspect of asymmetrical balance. The open sky must not rob the garden of intimacy, nor should trees, roofs, and eaves make too complete an enclosure. Open ground should be counterbalanced with groups of plants, rocks, and other features.

UNITY

Like balance, unity is central to the spirit of Japanese garden design. The garden must encourage its viewer to feel at one, not at odds, with the natural world.

Ideally, the form of the house and the apparently natural garden blend together. The dividing line between the two is softened by various transitional devices. Garden and house are also unified in sharing an enclosure that sets them apart from the outside.

Thoughtful choice and use of plants unify the design of the garden and contribute to its feeling of unity with the greater natural world beyond the gates.

Repetition also gives a sense of unity to a garden. Some plants and combinations of plants repeated throughout the garden, or in only one area of the garden, tie it together. The form of a mound may echo the form of a distant mountain. A low area in the garden or a background hedge may mirror the mountain's form. Angles, shapes, and patterns repeated throughout the garden unify it.

Stone is usually the greatest single physical unifier of the garden. Stones, in the overall patterns that they form, constitute the backbone of the garden. (See pages 52–53 for a discussion of stone and its uses.)

Water unifies, whether it flows through or covers a large area, or merely stands in a modest basin and captures the sky. Paths form lines that tie the garden together and invite the viewer to walk through and explore it.

Surprises create unity. Particularly in a stroll garden, bends in a path, a hidden depression beyond a rise, a shadowy glade, the arm of a pond that disappears among rocks and trees all lead the viewer onward and sustain a pattern of discovery. Even in a modest courtyard garden, the suggestion of a larger garden just out of view implies subtleties to be explored. The garden thereby has an appeal far greater than the sum of its individual parts.

Unity is also conveyed by complementary forms and qualities: the vertical and the horizontal, the bright and the shaded, the widening and the narrowing, the empty and the filled, the ephemeral and the enduring, the soft and the hard.

Unity lies in complementary forms. The vertical pagoda, trees, and bamboo screen balance low-lying stones.

PROFILE OF A JAPANESE GARDEN

Viewed from the highest point in its southwestern corner, this backyard garden stretches across the width of the property. Out of sight to the far left is the courtyard.

The main part of the garden—with a planted middle ground against the hedge—seems spacious. The house corner is covered in weathered bamboo.

A stone lantern atop a pedestal is surrounded by low junipers, variegated lilyturf, and Japanese maple. The ground cover is Corsican mint.

When the owners of the garden featured here purchased their home, they immediately set about creating a Japanese-style garden that would be harmonious with the house and entirely visible from indoors.

Designed to be viewed rather than strolled in, this small hill-and-pond garden with a courtyard encourages contemplation from viewing points indoors and from just outside the house. In the entryway and throughout both wings of the house, glass walls and sliding glass doors link the house and garden.

ENCLOSURE AND SITE CHANGES

Need for enclosure and privacy led the homeowners to build a solid fence around the outer garden area and to plant a hedge on the inside of the fence. Eventually the hedge became tall and thick enough to hide the fence and strike a balance between openness and enclosure.

The lawn that preceded the garden was essentially flat, with a gentle upward slope toward its west end. Soil has been built up near the southwest corner. A narrow mountain stream cascades from the high, forested ground there and slows as it widens into a pool curving around, then disappearing into dense vegetation.

The topography of this landscape looks natural even though it features a contrived illusion of expansiveness, with its long diagonal sight line and the enclosing hedge and plantings that obscure the middle ground between the garden and its surroundings. Borrowed scenery adds to the sense of expansiveness.

The plantings between the pond and the hedge work visually with the hedge to confuse the viewer's sense of depth and to suggest spaciousness. These shrubs and small trees obscure the surface of the area between water and hedge and combine with the tall hedge to heighten the effect of a three-dimensional woodland.

In the southeast corner of the garden, bamboo is used to create the illusion that the garden continues outward and around the corner of the house. In reality a fence encloses this tight corner, but the feathery bamboo disguises the fence, making the area feel more spacious.

FURTHER USES OF PLANTS

Smart plant use in this garden extends beyond creating the illusion of spaciousness.

Container plants add variety. Ground covers have created pleasing results in a mixture of colors and textures throughout the garden.

Other design principles contribute to the effectiveness of this garden's plantings. Unity and simplicity characterize the plantings, largely because of the owners' skillful employment of repetition and simplification. Only two varieties of juniper are used; their use is widespread, and their prevalence contributes a sense of cohesiveness. Other plants have been similarly repeated.

SPECIAL AND FINISHING TOUCHES

Poor drainage and, in the rainy season, resulting soggy soil required that the area beneath the living and dining room eaves be dug, lined with drainage material, and filled with stone.

The owners took advantage of this necessity by covering under-eave areas with cobbles to give the impression of the traditional Japanese drainage troughs that catch water from the roof. On top of the cobbles they placed a few larger stones. The troughs eliminate the need for planting these areas, and they create a pleasing transition from the strict geometry of the house to the freer forms of the garden.

Other transitional devices evolved over several years. Instead of letting asymmetric stepping-stones begin abruptly at the flagstone veranda, the owners now use a cluster of stepping-stones to start each of two small stepping-stone paths. One cluster consists of nearly rectangular stones that link the veranda with the irregular forms of the stones along the path. Similarly, careful shaping of the Japanese maple in the courtyard gives, from certain angles, a subtly squared-off form whose sides align with the sides of the house, creating another transition between the house and the asymmetry of the garden.

Not long after building the pond and filling it with carp did the owners realize the menace posed by raccoons. So they installed an unobtrusive metal grille just below the surface in one section of the pond. The carp retreat underneath it when threatened and, for much of the year, lily pads obscure it. It's a simple matter to control mosquito larvae in the pond: Overfed fish ignore larvae, but hungry fish eat them.

At some point, the owners found a worthy use for a prized porcelain jardiniere. Now inverted and nestled near the water's edge, it provides the perfect spot to sit and contemplate the garden.

Cobblestones under the eaves in the courtyard provide a graceful link between the house and the garden.

Shoji screens fold back to reveal a garden courtyard. Prominent is the aged Hinoki cypress.

COMPLETED GARDEN DESIGN

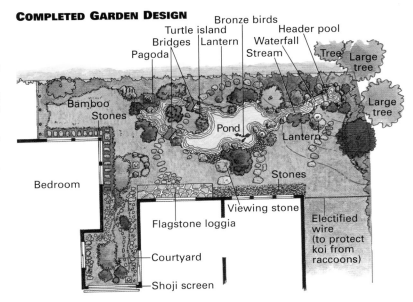

Bronze birds
Turtle island
Header pool
Bridges
Lantern
Waterfall
Pagoda
Stream
Tree
Large tree
Large tree
Bamboo
Stones
Pond
Lantern
Bedroom
Stones
Flagstone loggia
Viewing stone
Electified wire (to protect koi from raccoons)
Courtyard
Shoji screen

Front entrance

ELEMENTS
OF JAPANESE GARDENS

In a Japanese garden, earth provides the matrix for the basic garden elements: stone, water, and plants. These natural elements, in various forms and combinations, make the garden.

Stone, with its endlessly variable forms, serves as a building material, as a symbol for mountains and islands, and as stone itself, giving the garden its most enduring element.

Water, too, the Japanese find fascinating. To them it means purity. In one form or another, actual or suggested, water is the heart of every Japanese garden. Deciduous plants provide the Japanese garden with the transitory elements of seasonality, even as evergreen plants maintain the presence of life through the entire year.

Stone and water, in many manifestations and combinations, are the principle garden components discussed in this chapter. Each element is considered on two levels: the concept behind the element and its relation to the garden as a whole. Then the actual nuts-and-bolts installation or construction is discussed. Construction methods vary enormously, so methods best suited to gardeners in North America are emphasized. Specific guidance in using stone, as natural form or as building material, is given. Water features that are appropriate for residential-scale gardens are treated in depth. Ways of enclosing the garden and areas within it, as well as ways of allowing and directing circulation of people within it, receive close attention.

Choice and use of garden accents, those touches that evoke a tradition and a philosophy, are also included. Always, the spirit of the Japanese garden and the needs and resources of the homeowners are taken into account.

This retreat incorporates design elements, such as stones, water features, fish, gates, fencing, a bridge, walls, and garden accents.

WATER IN THE GARDEN:
WATERFALLS

I t is not surprising that in an island country with abundant rainfall, water figures prominently in gardens. A simple stone water basin can capture the magic of water as surely as a waterfall with a stream and pond can, and much more simply. A dry-water feature makes the viewer feel the living presence of water that does not actually exist in the garden.

Just inside the entry gate, low falls gently feed a pond that fronts the house.

WATERFALLS

A waterfall is nearly always the focal point of its garden, and no wonder: It marks a dramatic shift in topography. Usually it feeds a widening stream or a pond that from downstream viewing points leads the eye to the waterfall itself, always in motion.

Soothing water sounds cancel out noises beyond the garden and enhance the illusion of remoteness. You can emulate the particular charm of the natural waterfall by varying the seasonal volume of water, thereby reinforcing the mood of the season.

DESIGNING A WATERFALL: Most falls built in the classical Japanese manner consist of seven basic stones, along with any number of other stones used to enhance or extend the composition. There are many possible variations, including simplifications on the basic configuration.

The mirror stone, the central stone of a fall, in front of or down which the water flows, helps to determine the style of the fall.

The configuration of its lip—straight and smooth, or jagged—does much to determine the pattern of falling water. In some falls an arrangement of stones, rather than a single stone, functions as the mirror stone. The position of the mirror stone also affects the way the water falls. If the stone leans slightly outward, water spouts from its lip; if it leans inward, water flows down the stone, unless altered by volume and velocity. The mirror stone usually stands no more than 3 feet above the water level of the basin beneath the fall.

At either side of the mirror stone, standing up to a foot higher and somewhat forward of it, are the vertical, more massive flanking

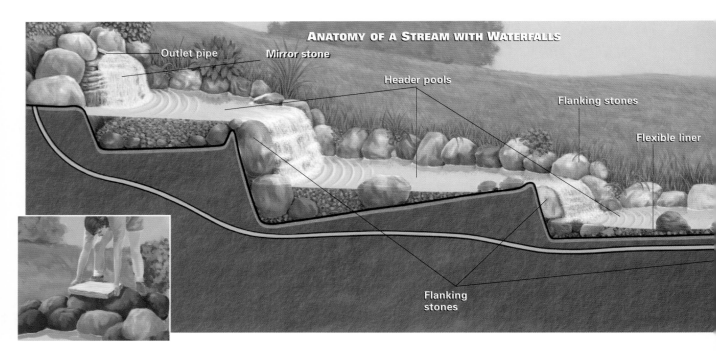

ANATOMY OF A STREAM WITH WATERFALLS

Outlet pipe   Mirror stone

Header pools

Flanking stones

Flexible liner

Flanking stones

stones. Usually these stones lean inward, toward the cascading water.

At the foot of each flanking stone, a base stone provides stability to the grouping by visually anchoring the vertical mass. Typically, base stones stand a few inches forward of the flanking stones in the basin beneath the fall. None of the pairs should match closely enough to be symmetrical.

Also in the basin, at its center, is the water-dividing stone, which deflects the flow of fallen water bubbling up from the basin. Against this stone the fall makes its sound. Typically this stone is roughly triangular in shape and points upward into the fall.

Knowledge of the basics of Japanese waterfall composition can help you design a fall that delights you. Always keep in mind the appearance, sound, and overall effect you are working to achieve. But do not hesitate to call in a qualified professional to check, refine, or complete your design. After all, it is usual for a Japanese garden maker to serve for several years as a master's apprentice before designing a fall.

CONSTRUCTING A WATERFALL: A built-up corner of the garden can offer the perfect site for a waterfall, suggesting as it does an unseen stream or other water source. You

The central stone of the fall, also called the mirror stone, stands no more than 3 feet above the water level of the basin.

might consider using a sturdy garden boundary wall at the corner of your garden to suggest, from inside, a landscape that continues upward and outward. Wherever you position the waterfall, allow space for a small reservoir at the top, behind the mirror stone, from which water flows out in a narrow channel or a broad sheet to the lip of the mirror stone. Otherwise, water flowing directly from the hidden pipe from the recirculating pump will gush across the top of the mirror stone and outward, rather than spread and drop in the style you intend.

Construction of the base of all but the smallest waterfalls requires the lifting and precise placement of heavy stones. Call in a qualified contractor unless you are confident that you can handle the work.

A torrent of water rushes over a series of falls past bronze cranes, blocking outside noise.

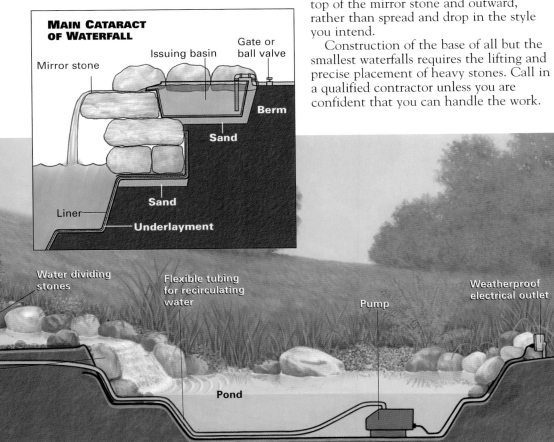

MAIN CATARACT OF WATERFALL

Mirror stone
Issuing basin
Gate or ball valve
Berm
Sand
Sand
Liner
Underlayment

Water dividing stones
Flexible tubing for recirculating water
Pump
Weatherproof electrical outlet
Pond

WATER IN THE GARDEN:
STREAMS

A low waterfall feeds a narrow stream, subtly accented by green plantings and moss-covered stones.

Whether streams link a waterfall or a simulated spring with a pond, or function by themselves in the garden, they have a particular vitality.
DESIGNING A STREAM: The basic considerations in laying out a stream are the scale of the garden and of any other connected water features, the nature of the topography, and the volume of water. A natural stream is a boon to the garden maker. But for most, the water source will nearly always be a domestic water system. The volume of flow will be determined by the efficiency and power of a recirculating pump system. A given volume of water may rush or drift, depending upon slope and stream width. Depending on how it has been laid out, a stream of a given volume may have both rapids and quiet pools.

As with other aspects of a Japanese garden, streams with turns and irregularities corresponding to the topography suggest nature more convincingly than would a canal that functions like a sluice.

As you begin your design, consider the following aspects of the behavior of a stream. Water flows faster in a narrow channel, slower in a broad one. Slope affects the velocity of water. A slope of at least 3 percent is required. A greater slope is usually desirable.

Stones may be used to create an apparently natural partial dam and rapids. Fast-flowing water makes more dramatic rapids than does water flowing slowly. Just below a series of rapids, a stone dividing the flow helps to create white water.

A turning stone placed in the water at the outer bank will protect the stream bank and bottom. Even if the streambed is concrete, the turning stone adds a look of natural stability and smooths the water flow around the curve. On the shallow shore opposite, some vegetation—perhaps an appropriate grasslike water plant at the water's edge—creates a satisfying balance.

For a natural-looking stream, choose unmatched boulders and place them randomly. On the insides of some curves, gentle slopes of pebbles look natural.

Rocks jutting from the sides or the bottoms of streams create interesting eddies. Any interruption in the surface of a streambed makes eddies, unless the water moves very slowly. A random scattering of stones in a stream looks natural.

CONSTRUCTING A NATURAL-LOOKING STREAM: Watertightness is essential to successful stream construction. Beginning at the source of the stream (the basin at the bottom of the waterfall, or the simulated spring, if there is no waterfall), make a watertight bottom. Dig and construct the streambed so that its depth, except in pools, will be between 3 and 6 inches, depending on the available volume of water.

Protection against leaks can be doubly ensured if the stream bottom consists of both

Where the stream narrows, the flow of water accelerates, then moves more slowly as it feeds into the mouth of the pond.

underlayment and flexible liner. This stream construction technique, identical to that for the pond bottom described on page 49, will support stones weighing up to about 200 pounds.

The streambed may be disguised or concealed in a variety of ways. Over the sides you can trowel about an inch of soft mortar, one small area at a time, and push pebbles into the mortar in random patterns. After an hour or so, use a paintbrush and water to smooth the mortar between the pebbles, making it less visible and more binding.

You can enhance the natural appearance of the streambed by spreading at least two grades of gravel (neither of them smaller than ½ inch in size) and some cobbles over the liner surface. Pebbles, gravel, and cobbles can easily be removed in the event that the paved bottom needs to be repaired.

INSTALLING A STREAM STEP BY STEP

1. EXCAVATION: If necessary, create a berm to give the watercourse the necessary slope. Compact any fill soil, or let it settle for three months. Mark out the watercourse with stakes and twine. Begin digging, creating any preplanned pools first, then the stretches of stream.

2. UNDERLAYMENT AND LINER: Install underlayment to prevent tears in the liner. Spread out the flexible liner, positioning and folding it as needed. For larger streams, you will need several sections of liner; overlap the higher sections on each lower one. Seal the seams.

3. PLUMBING: Position the pump in the pond at the opposite end from the waterfall or stream, where it will provide maximum water aeration. Attach the pump to piping in the pond and run it up along the stream to the outlet that you have roughly positioned into place.

4. TESTING: Turn on the pump and check to see how the water flows. Make adjustments by adding or removing soil under the liner.

5. EDGING: Lay a rough row of stones along the stream edges. You can mortar the stones to prevent water from flowing out of the streambed. Trim liner edges.

6. LAYING BED STONE: Disguise the liner with small stones, pebbles, and gravel in the bed. Scatter some among the edging stones, too, for a natural effect. Use as little gravel as possible because it tends to collect algae. Test the flow again.

7. REFINING: With the pump running, experiment with the placement of larger stones to see how they affect sounds and the water's splashing effect. Add or subtract stones as needed, or reposition existing stones.

WATER IN THE GARDEN:
PONDS

The most imposing feature of a stroll or a hill-and-pond garden is usually the pond. Nestling low in the landscape, the pond anchors the garden and its surface mirrors the sky, catches the wind, and often provides a home for fish. The rest of the garden is designed around it. The openness of a well-designed pond strikes a balance with trees, stones, structures, and land forms. The concavity of the pond creates a balancing convexity: Soil from the excavation may become a mound in the garden.

If a garden is too small to accommodate a pond, a water basin or a small pool can still reflect the sky and refresh visitors. Any garden can have a dry-water feature that suggests a pond as effectively, perhaps, as does water itself.

Choice placement of stones and construction of a stream and pond transform a plain yard into a serene world.

DESIGNING A POND: From the principal viewing point, traditionally the house or the veranda, a pond funnels the eye to the focal point of the garden, usually the waterfall, the mouth of the stream, or the spring that feeds the pond. The funneling function of the pond as it narrows and points toward its apparently remote source is another use of forced diminishing perspective, discussed on page 32.

Just as in nature, a pond has a source— a spring or a stream, perhaps with a waterfall; it also has an outlet. The garden should emulate its natural counterpart by appearing to have an outlet, even if it is nothing more than a small slope or a flat area with a few rounded stones and marsh grass.

Asymmetrical ponds look best, in keeping with the asymmetry of nature. Any asymmetric shape that works is suitable and should include a relatively narrow area section where a path can bridge the water.

CONSTRUCTING A POND: First, outline the pond's shape on the planned site. Use a garden hose or rope to outline a naturalistic, informal shape. Confirm the planned length and width using a measuring tape. Visualize the layout over the next few days, perhaps modifying dimensions or shape until you feel it's just right. When you're satisfied, use powdered limestone or gypsum to mark the final shape.

Marking the perimeter of a formal pond requires stakes and string to create straight lines, carefully measured angles, and perfect circles. Make rectangles or squares using triangulation. Use a stake to mark the center of a circular pool. Attach the stake to a length of string equal to the radius of the circle. Walk around the stake with the string outstretched fully, marking the circular perimeter as you work.

The method of construction described here, if followed carefully, should assure a perfect, durable seal.

Pond-building materials are more varied and easier to find than ever. In the past two decades, the quality of liners, pumps, filters, and supplies has improved dramatically. Although the lining and plumbing materials have been revolutionized, the basic tools remain the same. A spade, wheelbarrow, carpenters level, measuring tape, and a pair of heavy leather gloves are the basic tools you'll need to complete your garden pond project.

Prior to the availability of these many new products, creating any kind of water feature meant hiring professionals to form and reinforce a concrete water course, complete with plumbing and electrical systems. Flexible and preformed liners have replaced the concrete, and now you can install most water features yourself—without professional help—in an unending variety of shapes, sizes, and styles. Preformed liners are the easiest to install and best suited to small garden ponds.

Flexible liners are made from a variety of materials—polyethylene, which costs the least

A heavy lantern placed on a foundation stone echoes the weight and shape of the waterfall's flanking stones.

To play up a naturalistic setting, plants and trees are placed so they produce a lush look.

PONDS
continued

per square foot; polyvinyl-chloride (PVC), which costs more; ethylene-propylene-diene-monomer (EPDM), which is the most expensive per square foot. All flexible plastic sheets, they vary greatly in thickness, cost, and quality. As you might expect, heavier liners are more expensive, more durable, and more puncture- and tear-resistant than lighter weight liners.

First dig and carefully shape the pond. Its final depth may vary from 8 inches to 24 inches or more. Within the pond, the depth needn't be uniform. Local construction codes often limit the depth of ornamental ponds, so be sure to check the code before starting construction. Most important is a drainage pattern: Be sure that every part of the pond drains and that there is at least a 5-degree slope toward its lowest point, where the pump or drain lies. You may want to build an underwater ledge for supporting edging stones. The ledge may also provide fish with protection from predators. The bottom should be smooth, with no protruding rocks.

INSTALLING FLEXIBLE LINER: Lining a small pond is a one person job, but larger ponds require one or more helpers. First install a cushion layer for the bottom and edges of the pond. Called underlayment, this protects the liner from punctures. Sand is good, but it can't be laid on vertical surfaces. Old carpet works too. The material made

DIGGING A POND

1. Mark the outline of the pond with a garden hose or rope. Sprinkle a line of gypsum or garden limestone along the hose. When you're satisfied, live with the outline long enough to confirm the pond fits into the landscape.

2. Remove turf. Use it to fill bare spots in the lawn, or set it aside in a pile of its own to compost. If you have a large quantity, use it as the base of a berm or a raised bed. Stack it in place, then cover it with several inches of topsoil.

3. As you dig, keep the pond edge level. If it is not level, the liner will show. Check by resting a carpenters level on a straight board laid across the pond. Work all around the pond, checking every shelf and side of the pond so that there are no surprises.

4. Create a spot to overwinter plants and fish. In cold areas, you'll need a zone in the pond that won't freeze. It should be up to 3 feet deep and as wide as it is deep. Be sure this deep zone isn't in the same spot you want to place a pump or fountain.

5. Dig the shelf for the marginal plants about 8 to 12 inches deep. Position the marginal-plant shelf so that the plants frame your view of the water garden. Then dig a ledge for the edging as deep as the edging material and slightly less wide.

6. Toss the soil into a wheelbarrow or onto a tarp to protect your lawn. If it's in good condition, use it to fill in other spots in the landscape or to build a slope for a waterfall, or haul it to a construction site that needs fill dirt.

specifically for ponds, which resembles sheets of fiberglass insulation is optimum.

When using flexible liner, you'll find that folds and creases are unavoidable. As you fill the pond, you'll have to neatly tuck the liner—especially if it's made of less-elastic polyethylene or PVC—into uneven places so the weight of the water won't stress it unevenly and weaken or tear it. This will be easier if you let the liner warm in the sun an hour or two before you start work.

INSTALLING PREFORMED LINERS: Most preformed liners are made of either fiberglass or rigid plastic. Fiberglass is more expensive but lasts longer than rigid plastic. A 6×3-foot fiberglass liner starts at around $300, compared to about one-third that for one made of rigid plastic. On the other hand, a properly installed fiberglass liner can last 50 years.

Although installation is mostly straightforward, there are caveats to the successful installation of a preformed liner. First, take care to ensure that the liner is absolutely level and that nooks and crevices around the liner are carefully backfilled. If it is not, the liner is at risk of collapsing after it is filled under the weight of the water. Similarly, you have to be careful about using heavy edging, such as stone. Some liner edges are convex and unless carefully supported, the stones' weight will crush them.

LINING A POND

1. Cushion the hole with underlayment. This can be moist sand, old carpet, or underlayment made for water gardens. Cover the bottom and the sides. Cut triangles at corners and curves to help fit contours.

2. Position the liner. Let the liner warm in the sun for at least an hour to soften. Drape it loosely in the hole, arranging and pleating as needed. (This may be a job for two or more people.) Anchor the sides with bricks or stones, taking care to not stretch the liner.

3. Adjust the liner. Add a few inches of water to the pond to settle the liner. Pleat and tuck the liner, as necessary, to make it fit the contours and corners of the water feature.

4. Prepare for edging. Fill the pond with a few more inches of water. Adjust the liner, then fill to just below the edging shelf. Trim the liner.

5. Install edging. This can be flagstone, brick, cut stone, or other edging. Do a final trim of the liner. You can pat a little soil in behind the edging to conceal any visible liner.

DRY FEATURES

In this traditional Japanese garden, raked gravel appears to ripple as water would in a pond.

The design of every water feature described so far in this chapter applies equally well to its dry counterpart that only suggests the presence of water. Dry waterfalls, ponds, and streams, if they are well designed, have much the same aesthetic function and emotional impact as the water features they resemble.

WET AND DRY FEATURES COMPARED

Once installed in full-sized gardens, there are, aside from the absence of water, only subtle differences between dry features and the corresponding wet features. There is a significant difference in the construction for a dry feature—less earth must be moved and nothing needs to be waterproofed—and maintenance is easier and less expensive. An aesthetic difference, perhaps the only one that deserves comment, applies to ponds: A large dry pond, with its lack of movement or reflection and its unrelieved expanse, can seem glaring and unrefreshing. If you plan to make a dry pond, keep its scale modest.

RAKED GRAVEL

The material used most frequently to suggest water is fine, raked sand of a special kind. In Japan, decomposed granite particles are used. The surfaces of these particles are angular rather than rounded, so the sand can be shaped into the sharp ridges needed to maintain precisely raked patterns. Earthy, subdued tones make the granite more attractive than white sand as a garden surface. A very fine gravel might be substituted.

In this modern dry landscape, gravel acts as mulch without details, such as raked "waves."

CONSTRUCTING A RAKED-SAND AREA:
Well-packed earth is the traditional foundation for areas of sand; however, mud (which absorbs sand) and weeds are potential problems. You can avoid these problems by laying a porous-fabric weed barrier (one that allows water and air to pass through it) over the ground first and covering it with 2 to 4 or more inches of sand.

Raked patterns are usually stylized patterns of natural ripples, eddies, waves, and the smooth flow of water. Whatever their configuration, the patterns suggest movement, from a torrential rush to the gentlest purling or subtlest rippling around the edges of banks or stones.

MAINTAINING DECORATIVE RAKED AREAS:
Where there is little wind and no foot traffic, maintenance is minimal. Evergreen trees and shrubs do not make much litter. Under ideal conditions you will need to rake only every other week. Before you decide on a raked-sand feature, however, be sure of your commitment to regular maintenance: A neglected raked-sand feature is unsightly and out of keeping with the spirit of a Japanese garden. The Japanese use a special wooden rake to maintain the surface, but a steel rake can produce similar results.

Use the same decomposed granite gravel in dry river gardens as for raked-sand designs.

Less naturalistic than a traditional feature, cut stones mortared onto boulders act as a bridge over a dry pool.

Tree rounds form a section of retaining wall in a dry garden.

STONES AND BOULDERS

Stone is so important in every Japanese garden that it has been described as the skeleton, backbone, framework, and foundation of the garden. Above all, it is stone used as stone that has the greatest importance in the garden.

Even when used in groups, stones have individual characteristics, and the Japanese carefully select every stone for a garden. Graceful form, attractive color and texture, beauty of vein, and a patina of age are highly valued. Japanese history abounds with accounts of individual garden stones so beautiful that they became fittingly lavish gifts for rulers or booty for rapacious, powerful men of refined taste.

SOURCES OF STONES

Moss and lichen soften the hard edges of stones, rendering the naturalistic, aged effect highly desired in Japanese gardening.

The choicest stones bespeak great age and perfect naturalness. Weathered surfaces, eroded edges, and the organic embellishment of moss and lichen enhance their value. The severe angularity of a fine mountain stone pleases a sophisticated garden maker, especially if the surface has discolored or flaked, acquired some lichen, and lost the stark rawness of a similarly shaped stone from

a quarry. Local stones, or stones that resemble local ones so that they harmonize with the natural landscape, are preferable to fine imported ones that bear no relation to their new setting. Often, however, suitable local stones are not available, but harmonious imported ones are.

Unless you have easy, legal access to stones from the countryside and the means to transport them, you must go to a commercial supplier. Try to find a company that will allow you to choose each stone, at least each major one, and will protect the surfaces of stones during delivery. Ask if they use webbing or straps, which are available at drayage or rigging companies, rather than chains, or can put layers of wood or heavy cardboard between stones and chains or other damaging edges.

USES IN THE GARDEN

Bear in mind, as you consider stones for your garden, that a stone grouping often serves

Three boulders of varying sizes and shapes form an asymmetrical triangle, with sides of different lengths.

more than one function. A stone grouping seldom stands alone in the garden; to some extent it is usually combined with vegetation. In fact, plants are sometimes shaped to suggest or extend the forms of nearby stones.

Some stone groupings are practical. They may conceal a compost pile, a garbage can, or some other eyesore. Somewhat like sleeve fences, they may suggest divisions of the garden into intimate spaces. And like freestanding dividing fences, they may be combined with greenery to make a back-drop or a composition for a feature such as a prized water basin. Often they help to tie down a tall element such as a tree or soften the angularity of and anchor a freestanding fence or a stone bridge.

But, most important, groups of stones frequently serve as focal points themselves. They form or help to constitute mountains and real or suggested islands. Or they simply make naturalistic compositions, sometimes with abstract or symbolic overtones.

CLASSIFICATION BY SHAPE

The Japanese have developed elaborate classifications of large stones (boulders), but five basic shapes suffice to describe most.

Smaller boulders, sometimes called helping stones, fill out and lend naturalistic variety to a grouping. Standing boulders are either tall vertical, low vertical, or arching. A tall vertical boulder is higher than it is wide and is often the primary one in a grouping. A low vertical boulder may be of any height as long as its width equals or exceeds its height. An arching boulder may be lower than a low vertical; its top slopes to one side to create a wedge. The slope gives it a strongly directional shape, making it a dynamic component within groupings.

Two spreading forms are flat and reclining. A flat boulder is flat-topped and low, normally no more than a foot high. Stepping-stones are examples of flat stones of small scale. A reclining stone is also horizontal, but it is elongated and higher at one end.

STONES AND BOULDERS
continued

Modern gardeners are challenged by the harmony and character that are evident here, which is no surprise: The garden is about 300 years old and originally belonged to a samurai warrior. Note that the elements of Japanese garden design have remained the same.

ARRANGING STONES

Over centuries the Japanese have evolved systems of stone placement whose complexity and symbolic significance bewilder Westerners. The basic concepts are, however, straightforward and produce compositions of natural elegance.

Within particular groupings and within particular areas of the garden, use only one type of stone, to create the illusion that every stone is native to the garden site. If the stones are layered, arrange them so that their layering is consistent and they are naturalistically tilted, as though they were all projections of the same bedrock. Stones that appear to have been deposited by streams might justifiably look different, but even they should appear to be harmonious with the garden.

Avoid setting stones on the surface of the ground. Bury them as deeply as necessary to make them appear, and to be, strongly anchored. The use of smaller stones and plants around the base of the larger stones can reinforce the appearance of stability. For the same reason, use stones that are larger at the base than at the top.

Use odd numbers of stones. To the three primary stones forming a scalene triangle (see page 34) or other odd numbers of stones, add smaller helping stones. Groupings of five or more major stones begin to take on the proportions of large garden features. Unless that is what you want, limit a grouping to three major stones.

Consider the nature and scale of the garden, and select stones to suit it. The scale of a garden is suggested chiefly by its stones. A fairly large stone or two in a courtyard garden suggests that the space is larger than it is. The scale of the stones should determine the size of the lanterns, fences, shrubs, and other features close to them.

To create a landscape suggesting a particular land form, use appropriate boulders: vertical, angular ones at a mountaintop or the top of a waterfall, for instance, and rounded rocks along a gently inclined lowland stream or a pond. Focus on your overriding purpose: to suggest nature in simplified form.

Which side is up? Before you arrange boulders, study each to decide which is its best side. Determine its natural top, a matter of gravity, size, and, in some cases, the growth of moss. Usually the heaviest and bulkiest part of the rock is at the bottom. Moss grows on the north side of a stone.

STONES AND BOULDERS
continued

Japanese garden tradition classifies boulders according to their shape.

USING ASYMMETRIC BALANCE: The key principle followed in the grouping of stones is that of asymmetric balance, an understanding of which will ensure the success of your stone groupings regardless of all the other rules and principles, as long as you are clear on where the lines of view are for the arrangement. As a general rule, arrange major stones in threes, in a scalene triangle or an interlocking system of scalene triangles. Unless there is only one viewing point, think three-dimensionally, considering the depth of the grouping and its appearance from each viewing point, as well as its face-on appearance from the main viewing point.

Study your site, your stones, and your viewing points. Then sketch the possibilities that occur to you. Before you dig away earth to place the first stone, make a diagram. It will be helpful even if your plan changes while you work.

MOVING AND SETTING STONES: Where do you start? Which stone or unit of stones do you place first, to be followed by which one, and so on, not just in one group but in a garden area or an entire garden?

One method is to move from most to least important, an especially sensible sequence when large stones are limited in number and therefore should be used only in important focal positions. Another sequence concerns only groupings that are to include large stones to be placed by truck and derrick: Move from the stone or grouping most distant from the place where a truck with a derrick would enter the site to the closest, so the placed stones won't get in the way as the rest are being positioned.

Any damage to natural surface diminishes or destroys a stone's usefulness in the garden. To ensure that stones weighing several hundred pounds or more reach their final

STONE SHAPES

Tall vertical

Low vertical

Arching

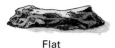

Flat

Reclining

STONE ARRANGEMENT

Basic boulder types are often combined, as seen in this arrangement.

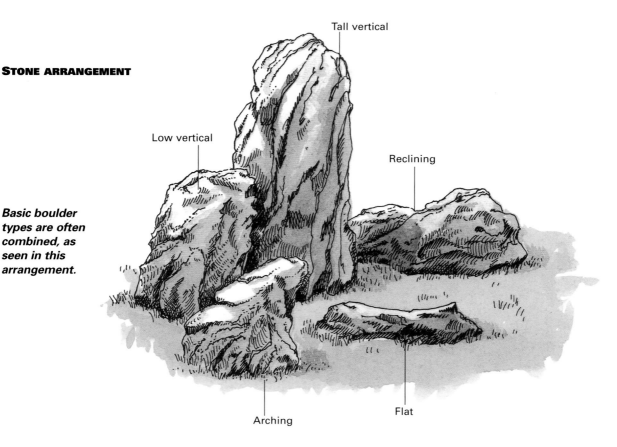

Tall vertical

Low vertical

Reclining

Arching

Flat

ASYMMETRICAL BALANCE: SINGLE SCALENE TRIANGLE

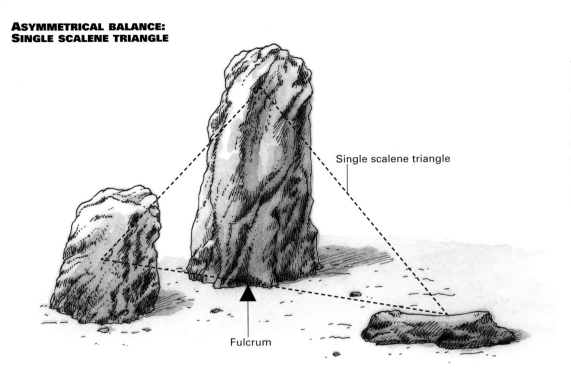

Single scalene triangle

Fulcrum

A scalene triangle is one in which all three sides are of different lengths. You can arrange stones in single (left) or interlocking (below) scalene triangles.

positions in your garden undamaged and in proper alignment, make some preparations. Unless you are adept at heavy construction, hire a fully qualified contractor, for your sake and that of the stones.

If you do the work yourself, use a wooden lever rather than a crowbar on any surface that won't be buried or otherwise hidden, to avoid scarring. Protect surfaces by using as much padding as needed. If necessary, use a block or a winch, or a derrick mounted on the rear of a truck.

Except in a dry-stream garden, where an unburied stone might suggest the continual shifting of stones by the force of the stream, bury each stone deep enough that it seems to be growing out of the earth. After careful measurement, dig a hole for each stone, and compact the earth inside the hole until it is firm and the bottom is at the intended depth. If the stone will be rolled by lever rather than lowered into place, dig away the earth on the side of the hole where the stone will enter, and replace earth as needed afterward.

ASYMMETRICAL BALANCE: INTERLOCKING SCALENE TRIANGLES

PATHS

With the exception of courtyard gardens, Japanese gardens invite viewers to walk through them. Stepping-stones in the outer tea garden lead visitors away from everyday concerns into a realm of quietude; the stroll-garden path invites visitors to set out on foot to savor the garden's subtleties and explore its mysteries. In any walked-in garden, a side path promises to reveal to the curious visitor a choice feature or other surprise.

The path, or a system of paths, provides firm, dry, safe footing; directs and paces the visitor; and protects planted, raked, or other prepared or detailed surfaces. If sensitively designed and carefully constructed, paths become not just the route through, but a part of, the garden's beauty and spirit.

Paths range in elaborateness and formality, from wide, elegantly paved stone walkways to stepping-stone pathways to the simplest of packed-earth trails. One garden may contain forms of all three. Changes of level call for steps, and wet or dry streams too wide for stepping-stones call for bridges.

TRAILS

The most rudimentary form of paths, trails require little effort or material to make. Their simplicity complements the naturalism of the Japanese garden. Trails that are both dressed and contained are far stronger architecturally and are thus less naturalistic.

BASIC TRAILS: These are paths at their most basic looking, as though the constant passage of feet (or hoofs or paws) has worn them into the earth. They seem nature's own creation. This is their chief asset in a style of

Bamboo holds back soil to stabilize steps cut into a gentle slope. The combination of gravel and bamboo is the essence of simplicity.

garden whose purpose is to suggest nature and summon its spirit. In even a highly crafted, formal garden, trails can lend intimacy to the quietest, most secluded areas.

Trails do have their drawbacks. In wet weather they become muddy; in dry weather they are dusty. Inevitably trails encourage the growth of weeds.

To make a trail, wet the soil to a depth of several inches. Allow it to drain, then with a hoe or shovel remove 2 to 3 inches of soil along with any rocks and weeds. A comfortable trail width is about 3 feet wide, but a variable width can regulate pace (walkers tend to slow down in the wide spots) and enhance the naturalistic feeling. Contour the trail so that water drains to the sides and away. Be sure that you pack the soil firmly.

DRESSED TRAILS: By dressing trails with bark, pine needles, composted sawdust, gravel, or crushed rock, mud is eliminated, dust is minimized, and weeds are reduced, although it is difficult to keep all dressings entirely free of weeds and fallen leaves. Where soil freezes, buckles, then thaws into mud, a covering is even more useful. All dressings need to be replenished periodically. Bark, sawdust, and pine needles decay; dry sawdust blows away; gravel and bark get kicked off the path.

Japanese in spirit, this path uses everyday materials, such as stone pavers, available at home centers.

A trail dressed with crushed gravel is bordered by partially buried river stones.

Gravel, with its rounded surfaces, provides an unstable footing if it is much more than an inch deep. Eventually gravel and even crushed rock will pack down into the earth, although a fabric weed barrier can retard or eliminate this problem, as will a generous layer of decomposed granite. Crushed rock (the ½-inch size) offers a firm footing. As it settles, pieces lock into place. In Japan the slushy sound of gravel and the muted crunching of crushed rock underfoot are considered delightful sensory additions to a garden.

CONTAINED TRAILS: You can install header boards, and make a more durable, less troublesome dressed pathway, if you aren't set on a trail that looks natural. A contained trail allows you to use a weed barrier or decomposed granite more neatly and easily, and it keeps most loose particles of dressing within bounds. You can minimize the formality of such a path by encouraging ground cover to hide the header board and make the path's width appear random. Or you can make a broad, formal gravel path (use ¼-inch gravel) contained by visible header boards, or by concrete or stone strips, as is done in many of the large gardens of Japan. When you lay out a trail, pay attention to contouring and topography to ensure that no puddles will form.

Aged stepping-stones wend through a moss covered corridor. Prominent spacing between each stone slows strollers so they notice immediate surroundings. The large lantern promises an intriguing vista.

STEPPING-STONES

Most popular in Japanese residential gardens are paths of *tobi-ishi*, or stepping-stones. Most stepping-stones are used on dry land, but they can cross streams and ponds. Some blend so well with their surroundings that they are

unobtrusive; others are intentionally fashioned and arranged to create formal effects. Sizes vary, but generally stepping-stones are between 15 and 20 inches across, requiring strollers to walk alone or in single file. Stone surfaces (smooth to slightly uneven) and, more commonly, the size, spacing, and pattern of arrangement permit the skilled garden maker to guide visitors toward a greater appreciation of the garden by directing their route and their pace as they walk through it. The design principle of hide and reveal may be achieved by this controlled pacing of the stroller.

POSITIONING: Space stones about 4 inches apart, closer if the stones cross water. Where you want to hurry the strollers along, space stones farther apart, but not so far that footing is unstable when stones are wet. Where you want the strollers to slow down, space stones more tightly. Similarly, uneven spacing slows the gait; even spacing usually accelerates it. Stones placed with insufficient regard for spacing and ease of walking will distract the strollers, making them feel as if they were playing hopscotch rather than viewing a garden. Determine the positioning of your stones before beginning to construct the path by laying out and walking over newspapers folded to the size of the stepping-stones.

STEPPING-STONE PLACEMENT

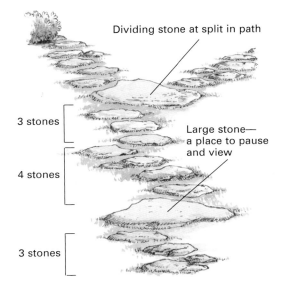

Dividing stone at split in path

3 stones

Large stone— a place to pause and view

4 stones

3 stones

PATHS
continued

Bury each stone so that it stands at the same height above ground level as every other stone in the path, somewhere between 1½ and 3 inches high. The top surface of each should be perfectly level.

Lay the largest stones first. As a general rule, let the largest stones span the axis of the path and the smallest lie away from the axis. Where one stepping-stone path forks or intersects another, place a large dividing stone to give visual and practical stability to the intersection. At sharp turns in the path, use large stones for sound, comfortable footing. Wherever you want the stroller to pause and look around, place a large stone.

Position every stone so that its length is perpendicular to the axis of that segment of the path. Not only will the stone look more stable, it will be easier to step on than if it were parallel to the axis.

In working out a sequence for stones, place together stones whose edges are almost but not quite parallel over the greatest length possible: a flat (or nearly flat) side next to a flat side, a convexity matching a concavity, a protruding angle matched to a recessed one. Of course, all such shapes relate approximately, not exactly. Wherever two stones cannot be placed together to match, add one or more small secondary stones, whose function is not necessarily to be stepped on but to complete the design.

The nobedan, *or stone walkway, zigzags, lending an architectural formality that contrasts with nature.*

STABILITY: Stepping on an unstable stone, even without accident, will interrupt the contemplation of the stroller. If a stepping-stone path must bear much weight (a wheelbarrow, for example), make it especially stable. And, to avoid discomfort and danger, be sure that each stone is set at exactly the same height above ground, as detailed earlier, or at gradually increasing or decreasing heights when on slopes.

Bulky stones set deeply and solidly into the ground will create stability. Beneath the 3 inches or less of exposed stone may lie 1 foot or more of buried stone. If you can't obtain such thick stones, anchor every thin, potentially unstable stone in a buried pocket of concrete. For each stone, dig a hole several inches deep and fill it with concrete. When the concrete has set, attach the stepping-stone with mortar, making sure that the surface along the path is level.

A far simpler and equally stable method appropriate to regions with mild winters is to put 2 inches of sand in the hole and tamp the stone firmly into the sand.

To ensure stability, stones placed in water, even in shallow pools, need to be positioned father apart than those on land.

PAVED WALKWAYS

Among the most elegant features of many traditional Japanese gardens are paved paths. Contrasting with the predominant naturalism of a garden, these paved stone walkways of a uniform, generous width add a formal, architectural note. A paved walkway may lie close to the house, at an entrance, or parallel to a veranda, or it may constitute a major thoroughfare across broad, open areas of the garden. Stepping-stones and trails dictate that strollers walk alone or in single file, while paved walkways are often wide enough so that people are able to stroll side by side. A uniform or nearly uniform surface allows strollers to pay less attention to their footing and more attention to the scenery around them. Variations on traditional forms provide endless possibilities for gardens.

MATERIALS AND PATTERNS: Whether laid out with parallel borders of granite curbing stone or unbordered, a *nobedan*-style path has straight, parallel sides. Angles rather than curves mark changes in direction. Many possibilities for paving materials fall within these formal guidelines. Patterns and textures may reinforce the symmetry or create random, natural effects that link the path with the predominant naturalism of the garden.

Most paved walkways combine stones of symmetrical and natural shapes. For example, large rectangular granite slabs may be combined with flat-surfaced river stones of random (or of more or less uniform) size.

A variation on the *nobedan* style is the walkway, or segment of walkway, consisting of two long rectangular strips of granite called label stones, because of their resemblance in shape to the Japanese cards, known as labels, on which poems are written. Laid parallel and nearly touching, the strips overlap for approximately two-fifths of their length.

CONSTRUCTING A *NOBEDAN:* Make a paved *nobedan*-style walkway much as you would the usual concrete walkway. But before you pour the concrete, have your pattern exactly planned and the components arranged on the ground close at hand. The largest components will have the widest joints between them, up to ½ inch.

Dig out the bed of the walkway, tamp or roll it, then spread a 2-inch layer of sand or gravel. Over the gravel or sand pour concrete to a depth of 4 inches or more. When the concrete has set, coat it with mortar and set stones and other pavers into it. Pave the edges of the path first.

Work on sections small enough so that the mortar won't dry before you set stones into all of its surface. Grout the open spaces with a dry mortar mix, then wet down the walkway; or work wet mortar mix into the open spaces, pressing the mortar down below the level of the stones. Grout that contrasts in tone with the stones sets off their beauty. (Grout coloring is available at masonry supply stores.)

An alternative method is to set the pavers dry on a packed layer of builder's sand, top it with several inches of "bank-run" gravel (washed stones ¼-inch to 6 inches in diameter), then sweep mortar mix into the spaces between the pavers and wet down the walkway.

This low, zigzagging plank bridge, or yatsuhashi, creates geometric order amid varied textures and sizes of plants and stones. The bridge also invites further exploration.

This path, a Western adaptation, retains the simple styling of Japanese design.

Threads of small stones mortared into the path complement the adjacent gravel bed. As an interesting but nontraditional accent, hoops of split bamboo form a border.

BRIDGES

High, arched bridges, originally designed to allow boats to pass beneath, are common to larger Japanese gardens. This one provides a tempting view.

Like stepping-stones in water, but often for greater distances, bridges extend a path over water or over a dry pond or stream. Build bridges of rustic, strongly naturalistic stone or wood, or a combination of wood and earth. A bridge usually spans the narrowest part of a pond, between opposing peninsulas, for instance, and usually reaches an island from the closest shore. A substantial

Built to suit the scale of a yard, this low arched bridge is ideally placed at an angle from the garden's main point of view.

bridge is used to span a thundering torrent. Still water or quiet streams need only a minimal bridge. The bridge should be positioned so that it is visible at an angle from the garden's primary viewing point, which is usually the veranda, rather than head-on or in full side view. A miniature, merely ornamental bridge is out of place in a Japanese garden, but a well-chosen, well-placed, and functional bridge greatly enhances the garden and provides vantage

points from which to view particularly beautiful facets of the garden.

STONE-SLAB BRIDGES: Bridges made of one slab of natural stone are prevalent in small, residential gardens in Japan. In the United States, however, their high cost and considerable weight make them less popular. This type of bridge sometimes requires two kinds of support: one structural, the other only for effect. The slab rests firmly upon large, securely placed foundation stones, which are mortared to the bottom and side of the pond or stream. Anchor or bridge-supporting stones, which rest at the edges of the bank next to the four corners of a slab, and match it in color, texture, and scale, are not actually functional, but they appear to support and stabilize the bridge.

A variation on the naturalistic slab is the hewn and slightly arched slab. Its arching is

This small bridge echoes traditional design but is easy for most homeowners to construct.

thought to lend a feeling of strength and stability. Often the area spanned is wide enough to call for two slabs, rarely three or more. Supporting rocks or rock piers hold the slabs securely where they join.

If you can't find stone slabs or want to avoid their considerable cost, substitute precast concrete slabs whose color and texture are subdued and stonelike. Because precast concrete slabs are heavy and unwieldy, you may want to call in a professional to deliver and set them into place.

PLANK BRIDGES: Heavy plank bridges are as simple and natural-looking as stone slabs. They may be used as slabs are used. Unlike stone-slab bridges, plank bridges need no anchor stones.

A popular style of plank bridge is the low, zigzagging *yatsuhashi* bridge. Rather than taking strollers directly across the water, the *yatsuhashi* bridge causes them to move slowly and indirectly, and leads them to contemplate the views to be seen as they cross.

Many patterns may be created with planks, laid singly or parallel. One example is a bridge of two parallel timbers, 4×4 inches, or larger, supporting closely spaced rails or boards laid across the timbers and nailed down securely.

A Japanese stone bridge usually has one slab; this variation uses two granite blocks—a style that often has rocks or rock piers for support.

Use pressure- or preservative-treated wood throughout. Where the supporting planks will come in contact with water or soil, cover them with some form of plastic sheeting.

EARTH BRIDGES: Bridges of wood and earth, called *dobashi*, are either flat or arched. Structurally they are similar to a plank bridge. For supporting timbers, use straight logs or curving ones to give the bridge a gentle arch. Cover the supporting timbers with rails—that is, smaller logs, 3 to 4 inches in diameter—placed as close together as possible and nailed down securely. For durability, lay 1 to 2 inches

of clay over the rails and pack it down. Make parallel 4-inch mounds of soil mixed with sand, spanning the bridge at its outer edges. Between the mounds spread an even layer of sand and soil, about 3 inches deep, and pack it firmly. Plant the mounds with a dense, low, perennial grass. Or instead of grassy mounds, use tightly tied bundles of reeds to edge the bridge. Another form of earth bridge can also be grassed over: Rolls of living turf are laid over the layers of clay and earth. Some earth bridges may be heavy enough to require trestles in the middle for support. Use treated wood wrapped in vinyl to ensure durability for the supporting portions of the bridge.

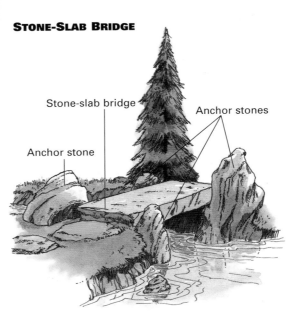

STONE-SLAB BRIDGE

Stone-slab bridge

Anchor stones

Anchor stone

Unlike milled lumber, natural log rounds used in this plank bridge reflect nature. If installing a stone-slab bridge is untenable, a plank bridge works nicely.

WALLS, FENCES, AND GATES

For privacy, for screening unattractive views, and for creating a sense of intimacy, a Japanese garden is enclosed and partitioned by walls, fences, or a combination of both. Occasionally earth mounds or trees and shrubs are used for screening or providing a backdrop. Some fences and walls make a solid barrier; others are open and merely suggest divisions or boundaries. Even the most solid enclosures, however, may have dips, gaps, or windows in them for capturing scenery borrowed from surrounding areas. In its appearance and its degree of visual solidity or openness, every successful enclosure or divider perfectly suits the style of the garden and serves its intended purpose.

Similarly, a gate is stylistically united with its wall or fence as well as with the whole garden. It may offer access to the garden with no sacrifice of privacy or may merely mark a division and provide a transition between parts of a garden, intensifying the intimacy of each part and the sense of mystery that a visitor experiences in looking toward a partly obscured area.

The boundary fence sets off the garden from the outside world. Woven bamboo, supported by a skeleton of milled lumber, functions as a screen. The stone foundation blends with the paving stones.

BOUNDARY FENCES

In Japan, boundary fences 7 feet or higher are commonly used to separate a garden from the outside world. They are taller and generally more solid, visually and structurally, than dividing fences within a garden. In the United States, local building codes may

The divider fence is more open than the boundary fence and defines certain areas, in this case the tea garden courtyard. Bound bundles of clustered twigs make a tall screen at right.

restrict the height of a fence and require a setback. But even at 5 to 6 feet tall, a boundary fence ensures privacy and sets the garden apart. A setback allows room outside the fence for trees or tall shrubs, which increase privacy, soften the effect of the fence itself, and from inside create the illusion that the garden extends further outward.

Aside from regulating views from inside and out, a boundary fence blocks wind, provides some shade, and makes an acoustical barrier whose effectiveness is enhanced with trees or shrubs.

The styles of boundary fences suitable for residential gardens reflect the simplicity and rusticity of most Japanese gardens and

WALLS, FENCES, AND GATES
continued

harmonize with the architecture of the house. Weathered planks, often charred in places and brushed or sandblasted to accentuate the grain, are frequently used. They are set vertically, alone or in combination with several other materials in any of many patterns, with or without a simple gabled roof. Other materials, used either alone or in combinations, include bamboo (constituting structural elements and panels fashioned in many different patterns) and plaster covering wood that has been faced with wire mesh, which is sometimes whitewashed but usually earthen. Some fences have a stone base, which may be up to 2 feet high, topped by fencing of other material.

There are many patterns for constructing a boundary fence, from the simplest to those with caps, roofs, or other ornamentation. The appearance of even the simplest fence is enhanced by a gabled roof. Your fence may be solid or have panels to create an open pattern. Horizontal planks or boards will increase the stability of the fence.

This detail of a bamboo fence shows artful twine ties.

DIVIDER FENCES

Within the garden, divider fences, usually smaller and more open than boundary fences, may serve a number of functions. Principally they set off or define a section of the garden, not by hiding it but by obscuring only part of the area beyond. They are usually low, between 2 and 4 feet in height, and usually 3 to 6 feet in length. Their open patterns make them gracefully light rather than massive. Solid fences are occasionally used to hide unsightly objects, such as heat pumps, or to make a solid backdrop for a garden accent, setting it off by providing an effective contrast.

Some dividing fences, such as those used as backdrops, may be freestanding. These need vegetation and stones nearby to soften their angularity and help anchor them visually. Others are attached at right angles to the house or another more solid structure. Attached, they are called sleeve fences; they are nearly always open in design, are made of varying materials (woven bamboo tied to the frame is most common), and have innumerable patterns. A typical sleeve fence is rounded at its outer end. The outer ends of longer ones may taper down to ground level. Sleeve fences create a transition between house and garden.

A weathered wooden fence divides a space and creates privacy yet is open to the air.

The roofed screen functions as a wall; it is made of lightweight bamboo.

WALLS

Solid, permanent walls surround many Japanese gardens. Costliest are stone walls, either mortared or dry—that is, carefully crafted of unmortared stones with earth between the stones, so that the walls can be planted with small-scale, perhaps trailing, plants. Mortared stone walls can double as retaining walls for high-mounded earth that slopes down into the garden. Shrubs may be planted on top for added screening, and rocks and even waterfalls may be situated there. Other frequently seen Japanese garden walls

A bamboo divider forces the viewer to incorporate the borrowed woodland scenery. Flowering dogwoods add to the illusion.

The moon gate and top rail, both made of laminated wood, merge into the boundary fence of bamboo screen.

are made of plastered clay into which straw has been mixed. Like boundary fences, walls may be capped by gabled roofs.

Many common building materials are suitable for making a wall with a pleasing Japanese feeling. Whatever material you decide on, remember that vegetation inside the garden can soften the effect of the wall.

GATES

Like fences, gates have their uses both at the periphery and inside a garden. Like fences and walls, they can be roofed even if the fence or wall into which they are built is roofless. Gates range in elaborateness from massive, double-doored outer gates topped with a tile roof, suitable for a large, formal garden, to a small, simply roofed, woven-bamboo gate separating sections of a tea garden, to twin, upright, bark-covered posts with an overhead branch crossing to form a gateway without an actual gate. This gateway will have a particularly Japanese quality if the ends of the crossing branch are allowed to extend beyond the posts, and the tops of the posts are allowed to rise above the crossing branch.

Gates should exactly suit the style of the fences within which they stand and should not be embellished with paint and bright or flashy hardware and ornamentation, which are out of keeping with the spirit of Japanese gardens. Outer gates are customarily secured with sliding wooden bolts. Gates intended to remain open should be fitted with discreet latches to prevent them from swinging free.

A traditional sleeve fence eases the transition from the angular house to the natural forms of the garden.

The delicate bamboo gate with a loop latch shows attention to detail.

The narrow gate with heavy sides and top suggests a special garden lies beyond.

GARDEN ACCENTS:
LANTERNS AND DEER SCARES

The age and character intrinsic to a pedestal-mounted stone lantern adds interest to the garden.

Japanese lanterns can be costly. Made of concrete, this one is attractive yet affordable.

Many traditional Japanese garden artifacts and embellishments are more than merely ornamental. Actually or symbolically, they may provide comfort or convenience. Especially in an American garden in the Japanese style, however, the presence of elements is justified if they merely enhance the garden's serenity. Using only a few looks best.

LANTERNS

Zen priests and tea masters popularized stone garden lanterns (*ishi-doro*) by incorporating them into tea gardens. Lanterns of stone (but occasionally of wood, bamboo, or bronze) are now the single most common artifact to be found in the gardens of Japan. Rather than light the garden at night, they are used to contrast pleasingly and subtly with natural features.

Even if not actually lit, lanterns are placed in the garden wherever light would be useful: along walkways, especially where turns or shifts in level occur, near boat docks (real or suggested), at gateways, near bridges or water-spanning stepping-stones, or near a water basin. They are also used to complete compositions of stones, or of stones and plants, to mark the edge of a pond, or to create reflections from an island in the pond.

The Japanese value the appearance of great age in a lantern. They have developed methods of giving a patina of age to new lanterns, such as smearing them with snail secretions or bird droppings and keeping them shaded and moist until moss or lichen takes hold. Occasional rubbing with dirt or humus may produce the same result.

Lanterns imported from Japan are sold in the United States, some for several hundreds or thousands of dollars. A graceful stone lantern nearly always justifies its expense, but a good concrete one of a rustic design makes a pleasing addition to most garden spots.

Clumped plants are the appropriate backdrop for an accent with intricate details.

Covered with moss, this stone wind temple resembles a naturally aged stone.

Although metal instead of stone, this lantern has a traditional shape appreciated by the Japanese.

If you want to light your lantern, insert a firebox of paraffin and a wick, or use a candle. Or, if you use a low-wattage bulb, you can wire your lantern. Cover the windows with rice paper or another, similar material.

DEER SCARE

The deer scare, or *shishi odoshi*, has its origins in agriculture: Farmers used it to frighten away deer or other animals that threatened their crops. Water flows out of a bamboo pipe and down into a lip reservoir, which is a length of bamboo set on a pivot. When the reservoir is full, the weight of the water tips the length of bamboo abruptly downward. With a loud clack it strikes a rock, the water tips out, and the reservoir swings back up.

In your garden you may decide to use a *shishi odoshi* near the edge of a pond, where the runoff can be channeled or will furnish the water for a tiny, intermittent cataract that would run down a rock face. A small recirculating pump might be used to provide the water.

The deer scare is decorative rather than functional. From a bamboo pipe, water flows into a bamboo reservoir set on a pivot. When full, the weight of the water forces the reservoir to strike the rock.

Hollow bamboo hitting stone creates a pleasant, mellow sound.

GARDEN ACCENTS:
WATER BASINS

L ike lanterns, water basins are nearly always of stone. The most highly prized are ancient ones of a simple, rustic design. The water basin, or *tsukubai*, appeared

Water flows from a bamboo pipe into a water basin. The Japanese maple, which overhangs protectively, makes the setting all the more intimate.

A lantern and an antique water basin with recirculating water create a feeling of calm and permanence.

At a Japanese temple, a drinking ladle rests on the water basin.

in Japanese gardens as an adjunct to the tea ceremony, to be used by guests for washing their hands and mouths in a ritual of purification before they entered the teahouse.

A typical *tsukubai* is low, requiring that the user stoop. A bamboo ladle often sits on the stone, and the reservoir in the top of the basin may be filled by hand or fed by a bamboo pipe that drips water into it. Even if the basin never fulfills its original function in a garden, its appearance, enhanced by the sound of dripping water and the rippling, reflective surface of the water, makes it a splendid accent.

Most styles are extremely naturalistic—a scooped-out stone is the most common—but some are more architectural. The more refined styles have names such as square star, oven-shaped, priest's scarf, and Chinese junk.

Surrounding the *tsukubai* are auxiliary stones that make a functional arrangement. In front of the basin is a stone to stand or kneel on. To its right is a stone on which a pitcher or kettle might be set. To the left of the water basin, a protection stone, nearly as large as the basin stone, shields the area from splashing water and may also accommodate a portable lamp. An underlying bed of gravel prevents muddiness.

In a tea garden, the water basin is placed close to the teahouse. When placed outside the tea garden, it may lie near the house, probably next to the veranda, where it would be taller. This type of water basin is called a *chozubachi*. In a Japanese-style American garden, a water basin may be placed wherever it is in keeping with its surroundings.

Like stone lanterns, authentic Japanese water basins are expensive. A well-designed concrete basin costs far less. To keep the basin filled, use a bamboo *kakeki*, or flume. Attach it to plumbing or connect it to a concealed garden hose. A small recirculating pump can also keep water flowing.

This modern, manufactured granite water basin is perfectly symmetrical.

An informal water basin, a boulder with a central depression, receives recirculating water from the bamboo pipe.

A concrete, rather than stone, water basin is pleasing and affordable. As an expression of unity, the gravel in this basin repeats the surrounding stones and pebbles.

GARDEN ACCENTS:
FISH

Fish add sparkle and movement to a water garden like nothing else. Before you stock your pond, however, there are a number of things to consider.

First, check the water. Ask your supplier what chemicals the water contains. It's likely to have chlorine, chloramines, or both. You can remove chlorine with a dechlorinator, or let it dissipate by allowing the water to sit for a few days. Chloramines must be removed with a chloramine remover. You can introduce fish to the water within 20 minutes of adding either a dechlorinator or chloramine remover.

Brightly and irregularly colored koi echo fall leaf colors, bringing life to the garden.

At a wooden bridge crossing the edge of a pond, koi have learned to gather for feeding by hand.

CLIMATE AND CONDITIONS

Plan fish purchases with your climate and your pond size in mind. Most fish do best in large ponds, because water temperatures and oxygen levels are more stable in larger volumes of water. Some fish do well only in cool water, others prefer warmth, and still others tolerate both extremes.

As a rule, the smaller the pond, the more tolerant of temperature extremes your fish must be. Water heats and cools with ambient temperatures; larger ponds are slower to respond to the changes, so the temperature is more consistent. For that reason, a pond that is more than 3 feet deep can house fish with a narrow tolerance for temperature change. But fish in a small pond—containing 50 to 75 gallons, or less as in a container garden—must be able to take extremes of heat and cold. A whiskey barrel half is adequate for one or two fish—as long as you choose species that aren't finicky about temperature.

Different fish do best at different depths. Koi need plenty of space in water at least 2 feet deep but often spend most of their time in the upper levels of a pond. The ideal stocking time is late spring or early summer, when the water reaches about 50° F. Although you can stock nearly any kind of fish in a pond, those bred for outdoor conditions will require less care and will generally do better.

WHAT TO LOOK FOR

Most tropical fish centers carry a wide variety of fish for ponds. Common goldfish are a favorite and are easy to keep, but there are more exotic—and costly—fish available. Oranda have heads with a "hood." Egg-shaped moors have exotic eyes that protrude on

stalks. Koi are a traditional favorite in Japanese gardens.

If possible, handpick your fish to make sure they're healthy. They should be young, lively, and preferably not over 3 to 5 inches long, with bright eyes and a sturdy body. They should swim effortlessly with erect fins and have no damaged or missing scales. Choose several small fish instead of a mixture of large and small varieties; small fish quickly become food for larger companions.

BRINGING THEM HOME

Transport the fish in a plastic bag inside a covered box. If the fish will be in the bag for more than 4 hours, ask the dealer to add oxygen to the bag. Even with oxygen added, don't leave fish in a sealed bag for more than 36 hours.

Acclimate the fish to the pond by adding about 10 percent pond water to the bag four times, once every 15 minutes for an hour. After putting fish in the pond, avoid feeding them for the first three to four days. Then, as they settle in, feed them daily, but never more than what they can eat in 10 to 15 minutes. Excess food will pollute the water. Most fish supplement their diets in summer with plants, mosquito larvae, and gnats, so you can reduce or eliminate feedings during summer.

Fish need shade and cover in the pond. Provide both with plants or bricks, stone, and other materials placed on the bottom or shelves of the pond. You should also equip the pond with an ultraviolet (UV) clarifier.

If your fish are hardy (hardiness varies, but single-tailed varieties are hardiest), they can overwinter in the deep zone of the pond, which shouldn't freeze. They will live off their fat reserves. All hardy fish can survive temperatures as low as 39° F as long as there's open water at all times for oxygen to enter and gases to escape. An electric water heater will thaw the ice to provide an opening.

In ponds that freeze solid, bring tropical fish inside when temperatures drop to 60° F. Keep them in an aerated aquarium or tub. In spring, after water temperatures reach 50° F, reintroduce them to the pond, and resume feeding hardy fish that wintered in the pond.

Acclimate fish to new water before releasing them by keeping them immersed in their travel bag for several minutes.

GARDEN
ACCENTS:
FISH
continued

Adding koi to a pond enhances the beauty of any garden. However, keeping these fish healthy does require time and special care, such as ensuring that water stays clean and at appropriate temperature levels.

COLORFUL KOI

One of the most refreshing elements that a Japanese garden can offer is koi. These brilliant relatives of the common goldfish, prized for their colorful patterns, are a kind of carp. Like a special garden stone, a magnificently patterned koi is considered a treasure, and such a specimen may cost thousands of dollars. The choicest forms of *nishiki* koi (brocaded koi) are too costly for most home gardens, but less costly forms are available. Given time and the right conditions, koi can grow to 2 to 3 feet in length and may live for decades.

Provide koi with proper pond conditions. Water must be effectively filtered and well aerated. Some fresh water must be added every few days, or continuously. If predators such as raccoons come into your garden, part of your pond must be deep enough, or protected by an overhang, so that the koi are safe. Determine exactly what special requirements your local climate imposes on the maintenance of koi in a garden pond. Partial shade is necessary, and there should be enough volume of water, along with ample depth, to prevent abrupt temperature changes and to keep temperatures low enough to prevent too rapid a growth of algae. If your pond does not have a biofilter, some other type of filtration system is necessary.

HOW MANY FISH?

To calculate the number of fish you can have in your garden pond, figure the total surface area of the water feature in which fish will be present. (This will give you an indication of how much oxygen will be available to them.) Don't count areas with marginal plants in the total, but do include the area covered by floating plants.

As a rule of thumb, each inch of fish should have 6 square inches to 1 square foot of water. (Koi need much more space—about 25 square feet for every fish.) Always err on the side of too much space. Use the table below to help you stock your pond.

2-inch fish: 1 square foot each
4-inch fish: 2 square feet each
6-inch fish: 3 square feet each
8-inch fish: 4 square feet each
12-inch fish: 6 square feet each
16-inch fish: 12 square feet each

If you provide aeration in the form of a fountain, you can add a few more fish. If you have a waterfall, which aerates the water substantially, you may be able to double the number of fish.

GARDEN ACCENTS:
MORE IDEAS

Traditional Japanese gardens are not highly decorated, although they may include symbolic sculptural elements in understated forms. As always, simplicity is key. Instead of amassing a variety of ornaments, consider a more restrained approach to make the garden a quiet, harmonious place. Choose accents imbued with some personal meaning that soothe your spirit. Position each ornament or decorative piece within the context of the garden's natural elements—stones, wood, water, light and shadow, and surrounding plants. In this way, introduced objects build the garden's character rather than detract from it.

Tucked behind lush greenery, this unobtrusive Buddha statue adds a touch of reverence to a Seattle garden.

Bamboo's smooth texture and subtle tones make it an elegant garden accent. Here, a cut bamboo stalk makes a unique plant container.

The striking outer gate to an inner garden invites both physical and spiritual passage across the threshold.

A round teahouse window suggests the moon. The bamboo grill provides privacy yet allows allows fresh air to pass through.

Gongs have an important history in Asian cultures, in both religious and secular contexts.

PLANTS FOR JAPANESE GARDENS

This chapter offers some basic principles of plant selection for a Japanese garden and instructions for giving certain plants the care they require. The gallery includes a broad sampling of appropriate plants, including traditional Japanese favorites and suitable alternatives. Although bonsai plants are not a feature of traditional Japanese gardens, a discussion of their adaptation, use, and maintenance in Japanese-inspired gardens is included.

Plants are nearly always a part of Japanese gardens, but their functions often differ dramatically from those of plants in typical Western gardens. In several respects, so do their placement, training, and maintenance.

An understanding of which plants are horticulturally and aesthetically compatible provides you with a basis for selection and planting. Practically and aesthetically, appropriateness is the key to sound plant selection and use. Reliable regionalized books and knowledgeable local nursery staff or landscape consultants can help you choose the most suitable plants.

Besides the basic, practical considerations of size, scale, and general appropriateness, there are aesthetic considerations. The shape and size of plants may, to some extent, be controlled; their color cannot. You will need to know the colors of plants (including shades of green) and their textures in order to choose knowledgeably. You will also need to know what plants and combinations of plants contribute to the Japanese spirit of restraint and subtlety.

The primary purpose of a Japanese garden is to suggest, through creating repose, universal harmony. Appropriately chosen and placed plants will support this purpose.

Nestled low in the landscape, a pond anchors the diverse plants that surround it. Each plant helps define the garden's structure and layers. Together the plants create a unified whole.

HOW TO CHOOSE PLANTS

Plants with varied form, texture, and foliage color give this garden a sense of depth.

Plantings, such as gold-green false cypress on the peninsula, accentuate the hill-and-pond-style. The maple tree echoes the hill shape.

Appropriate plant selection—both the species and the size of specimens—is essential to creating and maintaining your intended garden effect. Consider how easy or difficult a particular species is to keep at the desired size and shape. Planting design for Japanese gardens depends upon complete control over the size and shape of each plant. The quality of a garden depends on the plantings' being maintained at a certain scale. The smaller the garden, the more stringent the control will need to be.

In choosing, you must decide whether to plant a young tree or shrub and wait for it to reach optimal size before your garden reaches the form you want and whether you will be able to keep the plant at the size you want.

The overall Japanese garden plant selection is unified, and plants are used singly and in combination to give the impression of the natural world. This means they suit the garden and the places where they are planted within it, and groupings of plants are aesthetically compatible.

Appropriate in a Japanese garden is a gracefully naturalistic placement of plants, which are arranged as stones are arranged. Their apparent randomness looks more natural. Three plants used in a grouping are likely to look more natural than would two or four; a scalene triangle looks far less studied than an equilateral one, and certainly less than a row, a circle, or a rectangle. Observe the random patterns of plant distribution in nature before you arrange plants in your Japanese garden.

USE OF PLANTS TO CREATE ILLUSION

In light of the design principles discussed in the second chapter, you will appreciate that the selection and placement of plants have everything to do with how the eye of the beholder can be directed to focus on some garden areas or details and to gloss over others. Japanese garden design relies heavily on optical illusion, and plant use is instrumental in creating or reinforcing such effects.

BACKGROUND

Begin with an evaluation of the background greenery in your garden. In any garden the background screens out unsightliness. In Japanese gardens, in which a sense of apartness from the world beyond is usually a basic objective, not only is the world beyond usually hidden (with the exception of borrowed scenery, discussed on page 31), the background of the visible scene encourages the eye to move to focal points within it.

Because the eye gravitates naturally to dark spots in the landscape, evergreen shrubs or plants that create deep shadows will emphasize a focal point situated in front of them. The eye moves to the focal point and is held there by the contrast with the background darkness.

In a typical courtyard garden, and in some gardens of other Japanese styles, background greenery can delude the eye in a different

The focal point, a stone lantern atop a pedestal, stands out against subtle greens.

reinforces the shape of the stones—would interrupt the smooth, low middle ground and break the connection.

Texture and tone can also create or enhance the illusion of distance. Bold texture in the foreground and fine texture in the background stretch space; dark green in the foreground and lighter or softer tones of green in the background create the same effect by making the background seem part of a hazy, distant place.

Coarse-leaved plants in the foreground and fine-leaved ones in the background are used to make this space appear larger.

way. Its primary function is to suggest that the garden extends beyond the confines of what is seen, that there is more around the corner. A dense planting of tall bamboo toward one side of the far wall of a garden, for example, hides the actual corner, and the feathery foliage and willowy habit of the bamboo seem open rather than wall-like and final.

DEPTH

By manipulating the fore-, middle-, and background of a scene, Japanese garden makers use plants to deepen a cramped or shallow garden or make an already sizable garden seem even deeper. Large plants placed in the foreground with smaller ones in the background can create a forced diminishing perspective that makes the space seem deeper than it actually is.

This effect can be greatly enhanced by obscuring the middle ground. For instance, if you position a large Japanese umbrella pine in the foreground, near the viewing point, and a planting of azaleas and Japanese holly (comparatively small shrubs) in the background, you have set up a forced diminishing perspective, which causes the area to appear deeper than it is. But that forced perspective may not be very convincing unless you somehow break the smooth connection between the foreground and the background. The middle ground, perhaps a flat area of moss or ground cover, should include something that would catch the eye and further distance the background without in any way blocking it. Low, rounded stones interplanted with compact shrubs—for example, Kurume azaleas, whose shape

USING THE GALLERY

For heightened ornamentation, the red winged euonymus halos mounding golden cutleaf Japanese maple.

The section that follows includes, in several categories, plants suitable for Japanese gardens. The number of popular and appropriate plants is staggering. This gallery serves to suggest, wherever possible, at least one plant in each category suitable to each climate area of North America and to give a sense of the range of possibilities in texture, color, seasonal variety, size, and distinguishing characteristics. Plants are weighted toward species adaptable in broad climate ranges and include many traditional Japanese favorites. Also listed are a number of North American and other

non-Japanese species whose visual and horticultural qualities make them suited to various uses in Japanese-style gardens.

NAME

Plants within each category are alphabetized by their universally accepted botanical names. Each is followed by a pronunciation guide, which will will help you ask for the plant at a nursery. The most widely used common name of each is also included, though a few plants here have no common names.

Botanical (scientific) names are important because very different plants sometime share the same common name, and sometimes a plant has a number of common names. If you know the scientific name, which is unique, you can make sure that you are getting the right plant.

HEIGHT

The height of a plant is important in planning any garden. Because Japanese gardens rely heavily on maintaining plant scale to attain particular and overall effects, garden heights (as opposed to heights in the wild, under ideal conditions, or perhaps after decades or centuries) are listed. Garden heights are those that can be maintained by pinching or pruning. In each gallery listing, the height is noted first, followed by width.

SPECIAL ORNAMENTAL VALUE

To assist you in determining what ornamental purposes a species can (or cannot) serve in your garden, the gallery lists whether the plant has showy flowers, ornamental fruit or seeds, attractive green foliage, autumn color, or an especially appealing habit or branch pattern.

The short list of possibilities that you create for each location can be further refined by considering hardiness zone, growth rate, mature size, and landscape uses. The remaining sections provide additional information to help you finalize your choice.

Also, look around your region. Visit botanical gardens, arboretums, and garden centers. If you see an attractive plant that you would like in your yard, find out what it is.

When you have made your final choice, actively seek out examples of the plant in your region. If you can't find any, it could mean that you have stumbled on an

A foil of evergreens sets off the fiery foliage of a specimen Japanese maple. The tree, particularly the curving trunk, is an example of skillful bonsai training and pruning.

underused tree for your region, but it might also mean that you have chosen a plant that doesn't work well there.

Finally, keep your options open when choosing trees. If you have two or more possibilities, you can find bargains or switch to a second choice if the nursery is out of stock.

DECIDUOUS OR EVERGREEN

In Japanese gardens, as in all gardens, a key feature of a plant is whether it is deciduous or evergreen. Deciduous plants shed their leaves (or die back, if they are deciduous perennials). Evergreen plants retain leaves all year. Because evergreens are essential to the restrained color schemes and are the backbone of year-round greenery in Japanese garden design, many of the plants included in this encyclopedia are evergreen.

HARDINESS ZONES

Every plant listed is keyed to a map of climate zones published by the U.S. Department of Agriculture (see page 106). Zones are determined by an area's average winter minimum temperature, so the map is a key to cold hardiness.

TREES AND LARGE SHRUBS

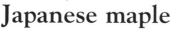

ACER PALMATUM

AY-sir pall-MAY-tum

Japanese maple

A weeping cutleaf Japanese maple with airy, threadlike leaves makes a graceful garden specimen.

- 10' by 10'
- Blazing fall foliage; deciduous
- Elegant, sculptural, spreading form
- Medium-fine texture
- Growth rate: slow
- Zones 5–8, depending on variety

Native to Japan, China, and Korea, this deciduous tree, called *momiji* in Japanese, is a must for the Japanese-inspired garden. Can grow to 25 feet tall and as wide with age.

USES: Japanese maple offers striking color, form, and texture. In Japanese-style gardens it evokes woodlands and forest edges, so it may be planted in the distant view. It is traditionally associated with villages and is therefore appropriate planted close to the home where it can be admired from a window.

SITING AND CARE: Grows best in morning sun, filtered shade in the afternoon, and cool, moist, mulched soil. Prune to retain shape.

RECOMMENDED VARIETIES: 'Atropurpureum' and 'Bloodgood' have deep reddish-purple leaves, red flowers, and fruit. 'Sango Kaku' has coral-colored stems and yellow leaves in fall. Cutleaf types have soft, wispy foliage.

Three-lobed leaves of amur maple are bright green in summer, then turn red in fall.

ACER TATARICUM GINNALA

AY-sir ta-TEAR-i-cum gin-nah-la

Amur maple

- 15' by 8'
- Brilliant red fall color; deciduous
- Bright red seedpods in summer
- Graceful, small habit
- Growth rate: medium
- Zones 3–8

A sturdy tree for the small garden, Amur maple is native to northern China and Japan. Unpruned, the tree can eventually grow to 20 feet tall and nearly as wide.

Uses: Amur maple adds texture and year-round interest to gardens. It is especially useful in small gardens as it won't outgrow the space allotted to it. Prune and train as a single-trunked tree or allow it to develop naturally, which usually results in a shrub-like clump. Plant individually as a specimen tree, or plant in rows to create a tall screening barrier.

Siting and care: Tolerant of dry and alkaline soils. This tough tree is also very tolerant of both heat and cold.

Recommended varieties: Both 'Flame' and 'Fire' produce especially brilliant red fall color.

AMELANCHIER X GRANDIFLORA

Ah-me-LAN-kee-er gran-de-FLOOR-a

Apple serviceberry

Springtime serviceberry blossoms are followed in summer by edible fruit that attracts birds.

- 20' by 20'
- Abundant white flowers emerge in early spring before or at same time as leaves; deciduous
- Red to purple summer fruit attracts birds
- Fiery fall color
- Growth rate: medium
- Zones 3–8

This naturally occurring hybrid between the North American natives *A. arborea* and *A. laevis* is a graceful, airy tree that provides year-round interest and edible fruit.

USES: Serviceberries occur naturally in moist or wet areas, and fit well in Japanese-inspired gardens beside a pond or stream. Or they can be used to evoke a woodland scene.

SITING AND CARE: Prefers moist, well-drained, acidic soils in partial shade.

RECOMMENDED VARIETIES AND RELATED SPECIES: 'Autumn Brilliance' has orange to red fall leaf color and abundant fruit. There are many other excellent varieties. Downy serviceberry (*A. arborea*) is a large single or multistemmed tree to 60 feet high with a rounded crown. Allegheny serviceberry (*A. laevis*) is a large shrub with bronze emerging foliage; its fruit is sweet, deep purple, and favored by birds.

CERCIS CHINENSIS

SIR-siss chih-NEN-sis

Chinese redbud

- 10' by 10'
- Deep rose flowers open in spring before heart-shape leaves emerge
- Glossy, rich green leaves turn yellow in autumn
- Growth rate: medium
- Zones 6–9

This densely branched, multi-stemmed deciduous shrub or small tree native to China and Japan has an upright, oval shape. It may reach 15 feet high.

USES: Allowed to grow in its natural form, this shrub implies a forest habitat. Choose a location where its spring flowers can be best appreciated.
SITING AND CARE: Best in full sun and well-drained soil.
RECOMMENDED VARIETIES: 'Avondale' offers a profusion of vivid magenta to deep purple flowers. Available as a single-stemmed tree.

Blossoms of Chinese redbud appear in early spring on bare branches.

CHAMAECYPARIS OBTUSA

kam-uh-SIP-uh-ris ob-TOO-sa

Hinoki false cypress

- 50' by 10'
- Soft in overall texture with spreading, relaxed branches
- Small, round cones
- Dark green evergreen needles with silvery markings on the underside
- Growth rate: slow to medium
- Zones 4–8

This pyramid-shape evergreen tree is native to mountain regions of

Japan and has long been an important Japanese garden plant.
USES: Employ as a canopy tree or use low-growing varieties to depict mountains and forests.
SITING AND CARE: Best in moist, well-drained, neutral to slightly acid soil. Plant in full sun to part shade.
RECOMMENDED VARIETIES: Numerous varieties available in varying sizes and forms, with foliage color ranging from dark green to gold. 'Gracilis' is a slender tree with nodding branch tips that grows to 20 feet high. 'Nana Gracilis' grows about 6 feet high. 'Crippsii Aurea' with golden foliage, grows slowly to 50 feet high.

Hinoki false cypress grows best with good soil drainage and protection from wind.

DIOSPYROS KAKI

Dye-OSS-per-us KA-kee

Japanese persimmon

- 20' by 12'
- Yellow to light green spring leaves change to reddish orange in fall; deciduous
- Edible fruit is showy on bare branches well into winter
- Growth rate: slow
- Zone 9

After changing color, the leaves drop a few weeks later, leaving the fruit clinging to the branches for

long winter display. Native to China and Korea. Can reach 30 feet tall and wide in time and with ideal conditions.
USES: Use for multiseason effect as a specimen or in a grove.
SITING AND CARE: Best in full sun and well-drained soil. Needs periodic thinning in late winter for maximum fruit production. Keep roots evenly moist to avoid premature fruit drop.
RECOMMENDED VARIETIES: 'Chocolate' fruit is flecked brown, with very sweet flesh. 'Fuyu' has golden orange fruit with firm flesh and is very popular. 'Hachiya' has good ornamental qualities; it bears large fruit that is sometimes seen

in the produce sections of markets.

'Hachiya' Japanese persimmon bears large, attractive, slightly pointed fruit. Foliage turns vivid colors in fall.

TREES AND LARGE SHRUBS
continued

A profusion of star magnolia flowers bursts into bloom in late winter or early spring.

MAGNOLIA STELLATA

Mag-NOH-lee-uh steh-LAH-tah

Star magnolia

- 10' by 10'
- Many-petaled, 4-inch white spring flowers before leaves
- Broadly oval small tree or large shrub
- Growth rate: slow to medium
- Zones 5–9

A small tree with a shrubby form, this magnolia is native to Japan. It can grow to 15 to 20 feet tall and wide in many years.

USES: An excellent accent plant when surrounded with perennials and ground cover to create a woodland scene.
SITING AND CARE: Locate it in full sun. Water in dry periods. Minimal pruning is required to maintain attractive shape.
RECOMMENDED VARIETIES AND SPECIES: 'Royal Star' bears pink buds opening to white flowers. 'Waterlily' is later flowering than the species and highly fragrant. Loebner magnolia (M. × *loebneri*) is an M. *stellata* and M. *kobus* hybrid. 'Merrill' is a fine, free-flowering tree with white blossoms.

The delicious scent of sweet olive permeates the air in spring, and again in fall.

OSMANTHUS FRAGRANS

oz-MAN-thus FRA-grans

Sweet olive

- 10' by 6'
- Glossy, evergreen leaves
- Tiny white flowers with powerful, sweet fragrance
- Blooms heaviest in spring and early summer
- Growth rate: moderate
- Zones 9–10

Native to woodlands throughout Asia, this dense, upright tree can reach 20 feet high and wide with age.
USES: Ideal for a woodland garden. Can be pruned to encourage upright growth where space is limited. These versatile plants may be grouped to create a screen or low hedge. Or use them individually as a specimen shrub. Where they are not cold hardy, grow in a container and overwinter indoors.
SITING AND CARE: Sweet olive needs fertile, well-drained soil. Grow it in full sun, but provide afternoon shade where summers are hot and dry.
RECOMMENDED VARIETIES: *O. f. aurantiacus* produces wonderfully fragrant orange flowers in autumn. The leaves are less glossy than the species. Related *O. × burkwoodii* is widely recommended.

The stiff, pointed, dark green needles of Japanese black pine develop on wide-spreading branches.

PINUS THUNBERGII

PYE-nuss thun-BERG-jee-eye

Japanese black pine

- 15' by 15'
- Large-needled evergreen with white terminal buds
- Easily trained into picturesque shapes
- Excellent for seashore
- Growth rate: fast
- Zones 5–8

Japanese black pine is tolerant of a wide range of growing conditions. Native to Japan, it can be a large tree reaching 50 feet at maturity.
USES: Traditionally used as a specimen tree in Japanese gardens, where it may represent the hills or seaside in the landscape. Prune to accentuate a desirable curving trunk and a well-defined, rounded head.
SITING AND CARE: Prefers well-drained soil in full sun. Prevent drought stress by occasional deep watering. Salt tolerant.
RECOMMENDED VARIETIES: 'Thunderhead' has heavy, dense, dark green needles and a dwarf, broad habit. 'Monina' (sold as Majestic Beauty) has lustrous, dark green needles and a growth habit like the species, but it is denser and more compactly shaped.

PRUNUS CERASIFERA

PROO-nuss sare-uh-SIH-fur-ah

Cherry plum

- 20' by 12'
- Purple-leaved varieties
- White to pink flowers
- Useful, shrubby tree
- Growth rate: medium
- Zones 4–8

A versatile, small tree, cherry plum is native to western Asia. Named varieties are preferred over the species. Can grow to 20 feet tall and wide.
USES: Use purple-leaved varieties with discretion as a color accent.

Locate plants to enjoy the early spring flowers that usually blossom before leaves emerge.
SITING AND CARE: A full-sun plant, it adapts to many soil types. Susceptible to many pests, especially cankers, aphids, caterpillars, borers, and leaf spots. Routine pest inspection is a must.
RECOMMENDED VARIETIES: 'Atropurpurea' (also sold as *P.* 'Pissardii') is the purple leaf plum. It has an upright, dense form and reddish-purple foliage. 'Newport' is a hardy purple-leaved selection. 'Thundercloud', another purple-leaved variety, bears pink flowers and has particularly dark, coppery leaves.

The pure white flowers of cherry plum blossom before the trees leaf out. The trees grow to 20 feet tall.

PRUNUS MUME

PROO-nuss MOO-may

Japanese flowering apricot

- 20' by 20'
- Spicy-fragrant winter blossoms
- Gnarled, picturesque form
- Growth rate: medium
- Zones 6–8

Among the flowering trees most cherished by the Japanese, this plant is more trouble free than other flowering fruit trees.
A broadly oval tree, it is native to China and Korea. It can grow to 28 feet tall and wide, but is easy to restrain with pruning.
USES: Locate it prominently so that the gnarled trunk that develops is easy to see. In Japanese plantings, this tree is associated with villages and deep woodland scenes.
SITING AND CARE: Best growth occurs in fertile, well-drained soils that are exposed to full sun.
RECOMMENDED VARIETIES: Numerous varieties with varied flower colors ranging from white to pink to dark red. 'Bonita' bears semidouble rosy red flowers. The flowers on 'Dawn' are pink and double ruffled. 'Omoi-no-mama' has semidouble, pink-flushed white flowers.

The ornamental, inedible fruit of Japanese flowering apricot follows fragrant winter blossoms.

SCIADOPITYS VERTICILLATA

sky-uh-DAW-pi-tis ver-tih-sih-LAY-tuh

Japanese umbrella pine

- 10' by 4'
- Small, refined evergreen conifer
- Dark green, whorled needles create umbrella-shape branch ends
- Growth rate: very slow
- Zones 4–8

Called *koya-maki* in Japanese, this native of Japan's steep mountain slopes has been gaining in popularity for its slow, restrained growth and easy-care nature. It can be grown as bonsai. Can reach 25 to 40 feet after many years in the wild.
USES: Often planted in Japanese gardens as a specimen tree. Be sure to site it with close-up viewing in mind, so its handsome boughs and striking mature form are easier to appreciate.
SITING AND CARE: Plant in moist, rich soil in areas where morning and midday sun give way to late afternoon shade. Provide some wind protection.

Dense and symmetrical when young, slow-growing Japanese umbrella pine becomes more open with age.

MEDIUM-SIZE SHRUBS & SMALL TREES

AUCUBA JAPONICA

a-KEW-ba ja-PON-i-ka

Japanese aucuba

'Picturata' is one of several varieties with variegated evergreen foliage.

- 6' by 5'
- Large, leathery evergreen leaves
- Attractive red fruit
- Adapts to dry shade
- Growth rate: slow
- Zones 7–10

Available in different leaf colors and patterns, this broad-leaved evergreen is native from the Himalayas to Japan.

USES: Does well in the shade of trees or buildings, and competes well with tree roots. Use as an understory plant combined with ferns, or plant variegated forms to add light to dark corners.

SITING AND CARE: Plant in part sun to deep shade and provide moderate water. Selectively cut branches back to a leaf node to keep plant from becoming leggy and open. Separate male and female plants are needed to set fruit. Variegated forms maintain their color best in open sites.

RECOMMENDED VARIETIES: 'Mr. Goldstrike', a male, has prominent gold markings on the leaves. 'Picturata', a female, has leaves with a central golden blotch and are yellow-spotted within the margin. Many other named varieties are available.

CAMELLIA JAPONICA

ka-MEAL-ee-a ja-PON-i-ka

Japanese camellia

Bloom time of common camellias ranges from November to May, depending on variety.

- 10' by 6'
- Evergreen foliage
- Blooms winter to early spring
- Often pyramidal
- Growth rate: slow
- Zones 8–10

Camellias bear large flowers in shades of white to red against lustrous, dark green leaves. Called *yabu tsubaki* in Japanese, this camellia is among the most representative Japanese garden plants. It is native to China and Japan.

USES: A fine specimen plant, or use grouped in a shady garden. It combines well with other broad-leaved evergreens, such as rhododendron. Can be grown in containers.

SITING AND CARE: Grow in slightly acid soil high in organic matter. Avoid overfertilization, salt buildup, and cultivation around shallow roots. No pruning is usually needed except to remove dead wood in spring.

RECOMMENDED VARIETIES: 'Debutante' is light pink, double, and early flowering. 'Daikagura', also early to bloom, has large, peony-type, rose-red flowers. 'Governor Mouton' has variegated red and white blossoms, and cold hardy flower buds, an advantage where spring frost occurs. 'Forest Green' (left) blooms midspring.

ILEX CRENATA

EYE-leks kren-AH-ta

Japanese holly

Japanese holly, a small-leaved evergreen with a naturally rounded form, adapts well to shaping.

- 10' by 12'
- Lustrous, dark evergreen foliage and delicate flower in late winter to spring
- Neat, rounded shape
- Fine texture
- Growth rate: slow
- Zones 6–10, some varieties to Zone 5

Called *inutsuge* in Japanese, this shrub has a dense, erect form with narrow, fine-toothed leaves. It is native to the mountains of Japan.

USES: In Japan it is often planted near water or as an understory plant. Or plant it in groups to give the garden mass.

SITING AND CARE: It prefers moist but well-drained, slightly acidic soil in sun or shade. Pollution tolerant. To shape, prune after new growth matures in spring.

RECOMMENDED VARIETIES: Numerous varieties include 'Beehive', a rounded dwarf plant with bright green foliage. 'Convexa' has small convex leaves that sparkle and is hardy to Zone 6. 'Dwarf Pagoda' is a picturesque dwarf with closely packed leaves, suitable for bonsai. 'Glory' has small, flat leaves and is unusually cold hardy, to Zone 5. 'Helleri' has small leaves and is very dwarf, 2 to 3 feet high. 'Hetzii' is similar to 'Convexa' but with larger leaves; hardy to Zone 6. 'Microphylla' has small leaves.

MAHONIA BEALEI

Ma-HOH-nee-a BAY-lee-eye

Leatherleaf mahonia

- 7' by 6'
- Leathery, spiny, hollylike evergreen leaves
- Large clusters of fragrant yellow flowers
- Grapelike fruit clusters
- Growth rate: slow
- Zones 6–10

This distinguished plant, native to China, looks good all year. A strong pattern of vertical stems and tropical-looking leaves provides structural interest.

USES: Plant against a stone, wood, or glass wall to contrast leaves and berries for a dramatic effect.

SITING AND CARE: Prefers a slightly shady, protected spot in the garden. Plant in rich, moist soil and give it plenty of water. Consider its ultimate size before planting because it is difficult to prune correctly. Avoid planting it where its spiny foliage can scratch.

RELATED SPECIES: Oregon grapeholly (*M. aquifolium*) has a loose, open form and reaches 6 feet tall. Native from British Columbia to Northern California (hardy in Zones 5–9).

Showy blue fruits and large, tropical-looking leaves are the hallmarks of leatherleaf mahonia.

PIERIS JAPONICA

pee-AIR-is ja-PON-i-ka

Japanese pieris

- 7' by 6'
- Broad-leaved evergreen
- Upright habit
- Pendulous clusters of delicate pinkish-white flowers
- Colorful new growth
- Growth rate: slow
- Zones 6–9

Attractive year-round, this shrub blooms in early spring for two to three weeks. The new foliage is colorful, bronzy pink to red. Native to Japan.

USES: Use in a naturalistic woodland setting or as a specimen plant, or combine with other acid-loving, broad-leaved evergreens, including *Ilex* species. It is also well placed among azaleas and ferns.

SITING AND CARE: Plant andromeda in moist, acid soil, protected from wind and winter sun, especially in Zones 6 and 7. It seldom needs pruning. It sometimes has insect and mite problems.

RECOMMENDED VARIETIES AND RELATED SPECIES: There are many good varieties selected for colorful new spring growth, flower color, and overall form and size.

'Dorothy Wycoff' has dark red buds that open to pale pink flowers. 'Flamingo' flowers are deep red in bud, maturing to rose pink striped with white.

'Flamingo' Japanese pieris is an upright shrub with tiered branches.

RHODODENDRON SPECIES

Ro-do-DEN-dron

Rhododendrons and azaleas

- Variable size
- Beautiful flowers
- Rounded form
- Growth rate: usually slow
- Zones 3–10, depending on species

More than 800 species and countless varieties of rhododendrons and azaleas belong to the genus *Rhododendron*. Rhododendron flowers resemble bells, and azalea blossoms look like funnels. Most rhododendrons are evergreen, and most azaleas are deciduous. They originate from numerous parts of the world and from varied habitats, and they differ greatly in form and hardiness. Select plants for your garden based on hardiness, ornamental qualities, and size.

USES: Locate these plants where you can enjoy their spectacular flower color and sometimes fragrance. Although many are handsome out of bloom, during much of the season they are primarily background plants arranged in groups some distance from the house.

SITING AND CARE: Plant in well-drained, acid soil. In the South, rhododendrons need more shade than in the North, where light shade is fine. Keep them away from salt spray and out of winter sun.

Exbury azalea 'Mount St. Helens' produces large golden flowers as new leaves emerge.

SMALL SHRUBS

DAPHNE CNEORUM

DAF-nee nee-OH-rum

Clustered on the ends of branches, fragrant rose daphne flowers bloom profusely in spring.

Rose daphne

- 1' by 3'
- Finely textured evergreen foliage
- Perfumed flowers
- Low, trailing mass
- Growth rate: slow
- Zones 5–7

This spring bloomer is a very fragrant shrub. It is native to central and southern Europe.

USES: Use rose daphne as a small-scale ground cover, in a rock garden, in shady spots, near entrances, or in groupings. It looks good with rhododendrons.

SITING AND CARE: It performs best in well-drained, pH neutral soil, protected from hot sun and drying winds. Plant high to reduce chance of crown rot. Avoid moving it after it is established.

RECOMMENDED VARIETIES AND RELATED SPECIES: 'Variegata' has cream-edged foliage. *D.* × *burkwoodii* (Zones 4–7) has extremely fragrant flowers that open white; compact, rounded to about 3 feet high and wide. 'Carol Mackie' has green leaves edged in pale yellow shade.

HEBE BUXIFOLIA

HEE-bee bux-i-FO-lee-a

Boxleaf hebe

- 4' by 4'
- Tiny evergreen leaves
- Small clusters of white flowers in summer
- Rounded, symmetrical form
- Easily shaped
- Growth rate: fast
- Zones 8–9

Good seacoast plant; tolerates wind and salt spray. Native to New Zealand.

USES: Grow mainly for form, texture, and evergreen foliage.

As with most hebes, this variegated type is grown mainly for form and pleasing foliage.

Use as a background or border shrub. Plants can be easily shaped into a hedge.

SITING AND CARE: Plant in full sun along the coast, partial shade in hot areas. Plenty of moisture and excellent drainage are essential. Prune after flowering to keep the plants compact.

RECOMMENDED VARIETIES: *H.* 'Autumn Glory', a hybrid hebe, has compact growth to 2 feet high and wide with 2-inch, deep lavender-blue flower spikes in late summer and fall. 'Patty's Purple' grows to 3 feet high with purple flowers. Many variegated forms are available.

JUNIPERUS CHINENSIS

joo-NIH-pur-us chih-NEN-sis

Chinese juniper

- 4' by 12'
- Fine-textured evergreen
- Adaptable, low maintenance
- Low-growing forms
- Growth rate: slow to medium
- Zones 4–10

Of the many dozens of juniper species, Chinese juniper is among the type most often grown in Japanese gardens. It may be either a tree, shrub, or ground cover depending on the variety. Native to China, Mongolia, and Japan.

Many varieties of Chinese juniper are low growing and wide spreading.

USES: Use low, spreading varieties as ground cover. Well adapted to slopes and hillsides.

SITING AND CARE: Best in well-drained soil and full sun, but adaptable to average moisture and partial shade. Place them away from lawn sprinklers and in general avoid overwatering. They need little if any pruning but tolerate shaping.

RECOMMENDED VARIETIES: 'San Jose', with sage green foliage, grows 2 feet high and 8 to 10 feet wide. 'Skybrook Gold', with rich yellow foliage and arching branches, reaches 2 to 3 feet by 6 feet. 'Aurea' (also sold as 'Gold Coast') has golden yellow foliage and grows 4 feet high and wide.

PINUS MUGO

PIE-nus MEW-go

Dwarf mountain pine

- 4' by 6'
- Dark-needled evergreen
- Dwarf form of a large pine
- Bushy, spreading habit
- Medium texture
- Growth rate: slow
- Zones 2–8, except deserts

Forms dense, cushionlike, slow-spreading mounds. Take care to select reliably dwarf varieties of mountain pine if you want a plant less than 15 feet tall and wide. Native to the mountains of Europe from Spain to the Balkans.

USES: Use as accents in rock gardens, or plant in groupings for ground cover.

SITING AND CARE: Plant in moist, deep loam in full sun to part shade. To maintain a compact, dense form, prune annually by removing two-thirds of each young, expanding candle in spring.

RECOMMENDED VARIETIES AND SPECIES: 'Enci', 'Gnom', and 'Mops' are reliably dwarf varieties of the mountain pine. *Pinus pumila* is a very low grower that can spread as much as 10 feet wide.

Dwarf mountain pine is a shrubby, symmetrical plant with needles in packets of two.

THUJA OCCIDENTALIS 'GLOBOSA'

THOO-ya ok-si-den-TAL-is

Globe arborvitae

- 4' by 4'
- Bright evergreen foliage
- Dwarf form of American arborvitae
- Neat, geometrical shape
- Growth rate: slow
- Zones 3–7

'Globosa' is one of several compact varieties of the large, upright tree or shrub, American arborvitae, *Thuja occidentalis*. In the garden, it is a beautiful, slow-growing globe that may eventually becomes larger than 3 feet. Native to the eastern United States.

USES: Versatile plant is useful along walks or walls. Wonderful for the rock garden or a low hedge. Can be sheared.

SITING AND CARE: Plant in well-drained, moist soil in full sun. It tolerates alkaline soils and performs best in areas of high atmospheric moisture. It is low maintenance, but needs some protection from winter winds, snow, and ice.

RECOMMENDED VARIETIES: 'Little Gem', 'Little Giant', and 'Nana' are similar to 'Globosa'. 'Green Midget' grows very slowly to 3 feet high and wide.

Dwarf globe arborvitae grows very slowly to 3 by 3 feet.

VIBURNUM DAVIDII

Vy-BUR-num dah-VID-ee-eye

David viburnum

- 3' by 4'
- Compact, glossy-leaved evergreen
- Showy, metallic blue fruits
- Growth rate: moderate
- Zones 8–10

This large-leaved evergreen shrub forms a low, wide mound. Egg-shape blue fruits in clusters follow early-summer, small white flowers. Native to China.

USES: Useful as a ground cover or in foreground plantings.

SITING AND CARE: Plant in moist, well-drained, slightly acid soil, although the plant can adapt well to other types of soil. In hot areas, provide some sun protection. More than one plant is needed to ensure pollination.

RELATED SPECIES: Among the many viburnum species, a good small shrub for colder regions is Korean spice viburnum (*Viburnum carlesii*, Zones 5–7). Compact varieties of this deciduous shrub include 'Cayuga', to 5 feet high, and 'Compactum', a dwarf plant to 3½ feet high. Both produce fragrant springtime flowers.

The metallic blue fruits of David viburnum follow clusters of small white flowers. Leaves are evergreen.

PERENNIALS

ANEMONE X HYBRIDA

uh-NEM-oh-nee

Hybrid Japanese anemone

'Queen Charlotte' hybrid Japanese anemone blooms in late summer.

- 3' to 5' by 2'
- Attractive, mounded 2-foot-wide basal foliage
- White, pink, or mauve blooms in late summer into fall
- Flowers held high above foliage
- Long-lived plant
- Growth rate: moderate to fast
- Zones 5–8

Gracefully branching upright form, lobed leaves, and single or double flowers. Especially valuable for flowering from late summer until frost. Some varieties grow at a moderate rate, others very fast.

USES: A refined color accent to brighten a shady corner in autumn. Also effective planted in groups beneath high-branching trees.

SITING AND CARE: Grows best planted in well-drained, moisture-retentive loam in sun to part shade. Provide average to constant moisture. Does not tolerate wet soil or drought. May need staking.

RECOMMENDED VARIETIES: 'Honorine Jobert' has pure white flowers on stalks 3 to 4 feet tall. Flowers are smaller than those on other varieties. 'Queen Charlotte', semidouble, pale mauve flowers, 3 feet. 'Whirlwind', semidouble, large white flowers, 3 to 5 feet.

ASTILBE X ARENDSII

uh-STILL-bee a-REND-see-eye

Astilbe

Fluffy salmon red flower plumes of 'Aphrodite' astilbe rise above shiny, lacy, bronzy-green foliage.

- 1' to 4' by 1' to 3'
- Mound of ferny-bronze to green foliage
- Plumelike flower clusters bloom early to midsummer
- Flower stalks rise over foliage
- Growth rate: slow to moderate
- Zones 4–8

With an array of flower colors—white, pink, red, and mauve—and bloom times from June to August, astilbes are versatile and vital plants for shaded locations.

USES: Plant astilbe in drifts for masses of color and fine texture. Or grow as accents in waterside or bog gardens. Leave the dried flower heads in the garden to provide long-term form and structure. Select early-, mid-, and late-blooming varieties for a long season of bloom.

SITING AND CARE: Plant in part shade in consistently moist soil. Mulch plants yearly with compost to maintain a rich, organic soil. If necessary, divide in early spring before growth begins.

RECOMMENDED VARIETIES: Some of the many varieties include 'Amethyst', a late-bloomer with lavender flowers (3 to 4 feet tall); and 'Bridal Veil' (also sold as 'Brautschleier'), midseason to late with 3-foot white flower plumes. Japanese astilbe (A. *simplicifolia*) is smaller with cut or lobed leaves, not divided ones.

CHRYSANTHEMUM HYBRIDS

kri-SAN-theh-mum

Chrysanthemum

- 2' by 5'
- Exquisite show, autumn to frost, depending on variety
- Huge choice of colors, shapes
- Zones 5–9

One of the oldest cultivated plants, mums bloom in just about every color except blue.

USES: Unsurpassed fall color, especially effective massed in beds.

SITING AND CARE: Well-drained soil and full sun are essential. Easily transplanted while in bloom. Space plants 18 to 24 inches apart. Provide ample water and fertilizer throughout summer. Pinch buds in early summer to make plants bushier and to promote more flower buds. Stake tall varieties. Mulch after ground freezes in fall.

Chrysanthemums are a favorite autumn-blooming perennial.

HOSTA SPECIES

HOSS-ta

Hosta

- 2" to 36" by 6" to 36"
- Lush, bold foliage
- Lilylike summer blossoms
- Zones 3–8

Ideal shade plants in most regions, hostas are a large group of plants with showy, often variegated leaves that vary widely in size.

USES: Ideal plants for shady, woodland gardens. Use as ground cover or edging. Combine with astilbe and ferns to create interesting texture contrasts.

SITING AND CARE: Plant in dappled shade and moist, well-drained, humus-rich soil. Enrich soil with compost or aged manure prior to planting. Water until established and during extended periods of dry weather. Divide crowded clumps in spring when tips emerge. Trap snails and slugs.

RECOMMENDED VARIETIES: August lily (*H. plantaginea*) has light green leaves and large, fragrant, white flowers. 'Frances Williams' (*H. sieboldiana*) is blue-green with golden borders. 'Sum and Substance' makes a large specimen plant with huge golden leaves.

Hostas are shade lovers with leaves ranging in length from 3 to 18 inches.

PAEONIA HYBRIDS

pay-OH-nee-uh

Peony

- 2' to 4' by 3'
- Fragrant, late-spring blossoms
- Superb cut flowers
- Long-lived plants
- Zones 3–8

These long-lived plants are attractive all summer, long after the blooms of other famous late-spring flowers fade and disappear.

USES: A stalwart of Japanese gardens, peonies provide beauty for a lifetime. Substantial plants can easily stand alone but look grand surrounded with low-growing, fine-textured perennials. Combine with blue star (*Amsonia*) and false indigo (*Baptisia*).

SITING AND CARE: Plant in full sun to partial shade in well-drained soil enriched with compost. Plant in late summer or early fall, with eyes (pinkish buds on top of the root) 1 to 2 inches below the soil surface. Space 3 feet apart. Provide support before bloom time. Remove all foliage after frost in fall.

RECOMMENDED VARIETIES: 'Festiva Maxima' is an excellent double white with red flecks at petal's base. 'Kansas' is an award-winning bright red double. 'Krinkled White' bears single snow white flowers with yellow stamens. 'Sarah Bernhardt' is double pink with silvery edges.

The cerise outer petals of 'Gay Paree' peony surround blush-pink petals at the center of the blossom.

PLATYCODON GRANDIFLORUS

pla-ti-KOH-don gran-de-FLOOR-us

Balloon flower

- 3' by 1½'
- Ornamental, inflated-balloonlike buds
- 2" star-shaped flowers in shades of blue, violet, white, or pink
- Vertical profile
- Growth rate: slow to moderate
- Zones 4–9

Balloon flower, called *kikyo* in Japanese, has been planted through Asia for centuries. It grows naturally on grassy hillsides in China, Korea, and Japan. The coarse texture and vertical profile of balloon flowers combine well with perennials of finer texture and mounded forms.

USES: Plant as a color accent next to a grouping of boulders, or group plants under trees.

SITING AND CARE: Plant in half to full sun in well-drained soil, and provide average moisture. Tallest forms and plants in shade and in very hot regions may need staking.

RECOMMENDED VARIETIES: 'Mariesii', dwarf, 18 to 24 inches, is one of the best known blue varieties. Same-sized 'Shell Pink' (also sold as 'Perlmutterschale') offers pink flowers. 'Sentimental Blue' is less than 12 inches tall.

Clump-forming balloon flower, a vase-shaped perennial, prefers well-drained soil in sun to partial shade.

VINES

hy-DRAIN-gee-a pet-ee-o-LAR-is

Climbing hydrangea has lacy, creamy white flower clusters in spring.

Climbing hydrangea

- 30' to 75' and as wide
- Deciduous
- Creamy white flowers in late spring
- Growth rate: slow to moderate
- Zones 5–7

Creamy white flowers appear in late spring against a background of shiny deep green leaves. Flower clusters are lacy, with large blossoms surrounding a center mass of small flowers. The vine climbs by rootlets.

USES: Often used to cover masonry walls. Combine with English ivy to achieve an evergreen effect. Be patient for flowers. Even if you purchase a blooming plant, the vine may put all its energy into leafy growth and you may have to wait up to five years to see flowers.
SITING AND CARE: Partial shade, average moisture, and good drainage are required. Little pruning is needed, but trim away from windows on a regular basis.
RELATED SPECIES: Korean climbing hydrangea (*Schizophragma hydrangeoides*) has tiny leaves and trails attractively.

*par-then-o-KIS-us
try-cus-pa-DA-ta*

Boston ivy

In full sun, the three-pointed leaves of Boston ivy turn scarlet in autumn.

- 60' and as wide
- Glossy, deep green, deciduous leaves
- Growth rate: vigorous once established; grows 6 to 10 feet a year
- Zones 4–8

This ivy of the Ivy League covers the buildings of many northeastern universities, turning them into structures apparently made of vines and leaves. They climb like a rootlet vine by tendrils tipped with adhesive discs. Leaf color changes with the season. They are light green in spring, darker in summer, then scarlet in fall.
USES: Stays flat against the structure that supports it. The vine's blue-black berries come on red stalks and are apparent after the leaves fall. Autumn color is peach to scarlet crimson. Fall color is best in full sun, becoming pale yellow in heavy shade. Winter effect is a dense tracery of thin stems.
SITING AND CARE: Tolerates shade and drought. Takes sun, but reflected heat of south-facing masonry walls may inhibit new growth. Usually pest free.
RECOMMENDED VARIETIES: 'Beverley Brook', 'Lowii', and 'Veitchii' have small leaves on less vigorous plants. 'Green Spring' produces large, 10-inch-wide leaves on vigorous plants.

wis-TARE-ee-a floor-a-BUN-da

Japanese wisteria

Showy Japanese wisteria flower clusters reach 2 feet long.

- Variable
- Deciduous
- Impressively long clusters of fragrant purple flowers in midspring
- Growth rate: vigorous; grows up to 15 feet a year
- Zones 5–9

One of the best-known and most memorable flowering vines. Vigorous, sometimes challenging, it climbs by twining and requires a sturdy support. Despite its beauty, can be invasive.
USES: Fragrant flowers are purple, though pink and white varieties are available. Individually small flowers come in clusters that hang 8 to 24 inches long. Flowers open gradually, from the cluster's base to the tip. Smooth gray trunks are picturesque with age, sinuously wrapping around themselves.
SITING AND CARE: Needs full sun and moderate moisture. Plant near strong supports: wrought-iron or heavy-duty and maintenance-free arbors and arches. Prune after flowering, taking care to retain short side shoots off the main stem.
RECOMMENDED VARIETIES: 'Alba' produces white flowers in long clusters. 'Multijuga' (also sold as both 'Longissima' and 'Macrobotrys') features very long hanging clusters, to 36 inches. 'Longissima Alba' has white flowers.

FERNS

ATHYRIUM FILIX-FEMINA

a-THEER-ee-um FE-lex-fa-ME-na

Lady fern

- 1½' to 4' by 1½'
- Evergreen in mild-winter regions, deciduous otherwise
- Lacy, yellow-green fronds
- Zones 4–9

A vigorous growing, North American native fern with upright fronds that grow to 2 feet long.
USES: Excellent members of shady borders and woodland gardens.
SITING AND CARE: Grows well throughout most of North America. Takes full sun (in most soil) or partial shade. Needs moist, neutral to acid soil. Space plants 2 feet apart. Propagate by division in spring or by sowing spores in summer.
RECOMMENDED VARIETIES AND SPECIES: 'Frizelliae' leaflets are clustered ball-like along fronds. Japanese painted fern (*A. nipponicum* 'Pictum') has 1½-foot-long green fronds highlighted with silver and purple.

Finely textured lady ferns grow best in well-drained, organically rich loam.

CYRTOMIUM FALCATUM

sir-TOME-ee-um fall-KAY-tum

Japanese holly fern

- 1' to 3' by 1½'
- Large, shapely evergreen leaflets remain glossy dark green
- Bold-textured fern with open form
- Good container fern
- Zones 9–10

Japanese holly fern makes a handsome, dense ground cover in mild climates. Fronds are shiny, surprisingly leathery, and light yellowish green. They grow about 2½ feet long.
USES: Bold and coarse-textured fern useful in containers and for shaded borders.
SITING AND CARE: Plants tolerate drier air and more sun than many other ferns. Space plants about 18 inches apart. Avoid planting too deeply or crowns may rot.
RECOMMENDED VARIETIES: Fronds of 'Rochfordianum' have lobed margins.

Excellent in shade in mild regions, Japanese holly fern has bold, glossy, leathery fronds.

OSMUNDA CINNAMOMEA

oz-MOON-da sin-a-MOME-ee-a

Cinnamon fern

- 2' to 5' by 3'
- Hardy and deciduous
- Zones 4–8

Excellent hardy fern for cool areas and moist soil. Has two types of fronds: tall, ferny, green sterile ones, and shorter, fertile ones topped with clustered, spore-bearing, cinnamon-brown bodies. In spring, the unfolding sterile fronds, fiddleheads, are a regional culinary speciality.
USES: A good choice for a sunny, low-lying spot. It is ideal for planting where water stands, and at the water's edge.
SITING AND CARE: Plant in light shade or full sun in constantly moist, acid soil. Space 2 feet apart. Soil should not dry completely.
RELATED SPECIES: Royal fern (*O. regalis*) is typically 4 to 6 feet tall, but can grow to 9 feet and as such is one of the largest garden ferns. Its dense root mass provides the osmunda fiber used for orchid rooting media.

Deciduous cinnamon fern has attractive green fronds surrounding shorter cinnamon brown fronds.

GROUND COVERS

Prostrate glossy abelia is a twiggy ground cover with small leaves and pink-tinged white flowers.

ABELIA X GRANDIFLORA 'PROSTRATA'

A-BEEL-ee-a gran-de-FLOOR-a

Prostrate glossy abelia

- 1' to 2' by 3'
- Evergreen to semi-evergreen
- Pinkish-white flowers; rounded habit
- Medium-fine texture with lustrous leaves
- Zones 6–9

Easy-to-grow and pest-free plant spreads slowly and has pinkish-white flowers in spring and fall.

USES: Plant prostrate abelia to create a ground cover in a small area.

SITING AND CARE: Thrives in well-drained, acid soil with partial to full sun and average watering. Set plants about 2 feet apart and plants will produce a solid cover in two seasons. Experiences winter dieback, so prune dead branches in northern Zone 6. New growth returns quickly.

RECOMMENDED VARIETIES: 'Sherwood' is slightly taller variety, 3 to 4 feet high and 5 feet wide.

Bearberry, also called creeping manzanita, is an ideal choice for dry and coastal regions.

ARCTOSTAPHYLOS UVA-URSI

ark-toe-STAFF-i-los oo-va-ER-si

Bearberry

- 3" to 5" by 15'
- Leathery, dark, evergreen leaves
- Slow growing, drought tolerant
- Very low growing
- Growth rate: slow
- Zones 3–7

Native to northern Europe, Asia, and North America. Very popular large-area ground cover in the Pacific Northwest and Rocky Mountain regions. Lustrous leaves turn reddish-purple to bronze in winter.

USES: Cultivate for a slow-growing, fine-textured evergreen ground cover, particularly near the coast. Plant with rugosa roses and shore juniper.

SITING AND CARE: Because it tolerates salt, lime, and drought, bearbery is suited for a sunny location at the beach. Set plants from containers or flats 2 feet apart for coverage in two seasons.

RECOMMENDED VARIETIES: 'Massachusetts' and 'Vancouver Jade' form handsome mats and are resistant to disease. 'Point Reyes' is heat- and drought-tolerant. All have urn-shaped, pale pink, flowers and red berries.

Japanese garden juniper is a wide-spreading evergreen ground cover, excellent near the coast.

JUNIPERUS CONFERTA

joo-NIH-per-us con-FIR-ta

Shore juniper

- 1' by 8'
- Evergreen conifer
- Fine texture
- Zones 5–9

Short, pointed needles cover this 8- to 12-inch-tall plant. Fine-textured but sturdy and low maintenance.

USES: Excellent choice for Japanese gardens, especially those near the seashore. It has soft-looking but prickly bluish-green foliage and a dense, matlike growth habit. Light green leaves trail attractively over walls. Native to coastal Japan.

SITING AND CARE: Plants thrive in average soil and full sun. Protect young plants from cold until they have formed hard wood. Provide afternoon shade in hot-summer climates. Propagate shore juniper from seed, hardwood cuttings, grafts, or by layering.

RECOMMENDED VARIETIES: 'Blue Ice' and 'Blue Pacific' are more dense looking, grow ultimately to about the same size, and feature foliage that is rich blue-green. 'Emerald Sea' is valued for its brilliant green color.

MENTHA REQUIENII

MEN-tha rek-wen-E-eye

Corsican mint

- 1" by 18"
- Semi-evergreen perennial
- Very low growing
- Zones 7–10

Pungent, fresh scent of peppermint is released when crushed underfoot.
USES: Lightly traveled paths, perhaps growing in paving cracks and seams; also beside streams and ponds.
SITING AND CARE: Sun to partial shade. Shear or mow plants in winter before growth begins. Propagate by seed or division in early spring.
RELATED SPECIES: Many mint species and hybrids are available: Peppermint (M. × *piperita*) grows to 3 feet tall and is favored for tea.

One-inch-tall Corsican mint releases a peppermint aroma when crushed.

SAGINA SUBULATA

sa-GINA sub-u-LAH-ta

Pearlwort

- 2" by 18"
- Mosslike mats of evergreen leaves and stems
- Green forms are Irish moss; golden-green forms are Scotch moss
- Zones 7–10

Pearlwort is a European native plant that has the look and feel of true moss.
USES: Excellent for filling gaps between stepping-stones, pavers, and similar small areas.
SITING AND CARE: Plants need good soil, moisture, and drainage. They don't grow well in the kinds of conditions that suit true mosses. Limited foot traffic is okay. Be on the lookout for slugs, snails, and cutworms.
RELATED SPECIES AND VARIETIES: Irish moss (*Selaginella involens*) is similar but less common. Golden-green forms of both pearlwort and Irish moss are known as Scotch moss.

A lush carpet of pearlwort provides a striking contrast to stepping-stones and evergreens.

SARCOCOCCA HOOKERIANA HUMILIS

sar-ko-KOK-a hook-er-ee-ANNA HEW-mil-is

Dwarf sweet box

- 1½ to 2' by 3' to 6'
- Rounded evergreen shrub
- Zones 6–9

Sweet box is commonly used in Japanese gardens. It is favored because its leaves are neat and attractive year-round. Though flowers are not large, they are intensely fragrant.
USES: Plant sweet box to add form and year-round texture to shaded areas. Grows well in soil with many tree roots. Plant near doors and passageways to enjoy the scent. Combine with azaleas and other similar acid-loving plants.
SITING AND CARE: Sweet box needs moist, well-drained soil with plenty of organic matter. Tolerates full and partial shade. Growth is most vigorous and foliage darkest green in soil that is slightly acidic. Tolerant of air pollution.
RELATED SPECIES: S. *confusa* grows 3 to 5 feet tall and is a rounded, dense shrub that produces white flowers followed by black berries. S. *ruscifolia* grows 4 to 6 feet tall and to 7 feet wide and produces red berries.

Dwarf sweet box has outstanding foliage and inconspicuous but highly scented blooms.

BAMBOOS

Golden stems striped with green distinguish 'Alphonse Karr'. Lower stems produce fewer branches.

BAMBUSA MULTIPLEX 'FERNLEAF'

bam-BOO-sa MUL-ti-plex

Fernleaf bamboo

- 6' to 10' by 4', clumping
- Evergreen
- 10 to 20 tiny leaves per stem
- Thin stems
- Zones 9–10

A ferny look is created by closely spaced leaves and thin, reedy stems. **USES:** Traditionally known as hedge bamboo because it branches from bottom to top and produces dense foliage. Also because it adapts well to shearing.

SITING AND CARE: Loses its ferny look and becomes coarser if grown in rich soil with generous amounts of water.

RECOMMENDED VARIETIES: 'Alphonse Karr' has attractive gold stems striped with green and is more common than the species. 'Fernleaf' makes ferny leaves if given moderate water. 'Golden Goddess' has gold stems, arching habit. 'Midori Green Alphas' makes a fast-growing hedge up to 15 feet tall.

Rhizomes of yellow groove bamboo spread sideways unless contained by a root barrier.

PHYLLOSTACHYS AUREOSULCATA

phil-o-STA-kis or-e-o-SUL-ca-ta

Yellow groove bamboo

- 12' to 15' by 10', spreading
- Deciduous
- Stems up to 1½ inches thick
- Yellow stems usually grow in zigzag manner at base
- Zones 5–10, but roots survive Zone 4 winters under mulch and snow

A running bamboo with a dense, vertical habit. Young stems have yellow-green grooves.

USES: Excellent as a screen or contained specimen.

SITING AND CARE: Grow in fertile, well-drained soil but with ample moisture. Full sun to partial shade. Divide clumps in early spring just before new growth begins. Prevent spreading by installing around the containment area a 30-mil-thick rhizome barrier at least 2 feet deep and 3 inches above ground.

RECOMMENDED VARIETIES: *P. a. aureocaulis* stems are sulfur yellow. 'Spectabilis' has thick, yellow stems with green stripes.

PHYLLOSTACHYS NIGRA

phil-o-STA-kis NI-gra

Black bamboo

- 4' to 8' by 4', clumping
- Deciduous
- Arching golden stems turning ebony black after 2 to 3 years
- Best contained; mildly spreading
- Zones 7–10

This is one of the most striking bamboos, with its bright green leaves and black-speckled stems. **USES:** Excellent screen or barrier planting. Does well in containers. Can come indoors in winter where not hardy.

SITING AND CARE: Grow in fertile, well-drained soil but with ample moisture. Full sun to partial shade. To propagate, divide clumps in early spring just before new growth begins. Excellent container plant partly because spreading is naturally restrained. Plant where spread is naturally limited, or establish barrier at planting time.

RECOMMENDED VARIETIES: 'Boryana' has green to yellow-green stems with purplish spots. *P. n. henonis* is larger and with white stems. Golden stems of *P. sulphurea* 'Robert Young' have green stripes.

A favorite Japanese garden ornamental, black bamboo provides striking color and graceful form.

PLEIOBLASTUS AURICOMUS

plee-o-BLAST-us aw-rik-O-mus

Dwarf greenstripe

- 1' to 3', spreading
- Deciduous
- Leaves 1' by 7", hairy underneath
- Stems purplish-green
- Zones 5–10

Spreading, but relatively less aggressively than others of its type.
USES: Excellent ground cover or container plant in shady areas.
SITING AND CARE: Grow in fertile, rich, and well-drained soil in partial shade. Divide clumps in spring before growth begins. Plant only where contained by in-soil barriers that can block spreading. Mow annually to refresh growth.
RELATED SPECIES: *P. variegatus* offers white variegated leaves. It grows 3 feet high and is deciduous but hardy to Zone 4. Simon bamboo (*P. simonii*) is taller, to 15 feet, and is a very aggressive spreader best restrained to a container. It's hardy to Zone 6. Note: *P. auricomus* is also sold as *Arundinaria auricoma*.

Green and gold leaves grace diminutive, though aggressive, dwarf greenstripe.

PLEIOBLASTUS PYGMAEUS

plee-o-BLAST-us pig-MAY-us

Pygmy bamboo

- 6" to 12", spreading
- Leaves are slightly hairy
- Zones 7–10

A bushy, aggressive running bamboo with bright green leaves.
USES: Upright-growing and very dwarf bamboo. Aggressive spreader good for containers, where paving restricts growth, and possibly bank erosion control.

SITING AND CARE: Grow in fertile, rich and well-drained soil. Full sun to partial shade. Divide clumps in spring before growth begins. Mow or cut back to ground in early spring to force fresh new leaves.
RECOMMENDED VARIETIES: *P. p. distichus* has hollow stems and hairless leaves. Note: Pygmy bamboo is also sold as both *Arundinaria pygmaea* and *Sasa pygmaea*.

Yellow-green pygmy bamboo is an attractive small-area ground cover.

SASA VEITCHII

SA-sa VETCH-ee-eye

Kuma bamboo grass

- 2' to 4', spreading
- Deciduous
- Smooth, cylindrical canes have waxy coating
- Zones 7–10

Native to moist woodlands in Japan, this rampant spreader has 10-inch, dark green leaves. In late fall and winter, leaves have precisely delineated, cream-colored edges, creating a subtle effect.
USES: An excellent ground cover in large areas, or restrain with a root barrier and use as an accent in a small space.
SITING AND CARE: Grow in fertile, moist, well-drained soil in full sun to partial shade. Propagate by division in spring. Excellent in containers, and often preferred as a natural way to restrain rampant spreading.
RELATED SPECIES: *S. palmata* has purple-streaked stems and bright green leaves. Note: *Sasa veitchii* is also sold as *Sasa albomarginata*.

The leaf margins of Kuma bamboo grass turn from green to cream in autumn and winter.

WATER PLANTS

Semi-evergreen, grasslike foliage of 'Ogon' Japanese sweet flag has golden-yellow variegation.

ACORUS GRAMINEUS

a-CORE-us gra-MIN-ee-us

Japanese sweet flag

- 12 to 18" tall by 18" wide
- Semi-evergreen to deciduous
- Narrow leaves form sculptural tufts
- Neat and pest-free plant
- Zones 6–10

Native throughout Northern Hemisphere. Related to calla lily, but the flower is inconspicuous without the colorful bract.

USES: Excellent foliage plant for the shallow margins of a pool or stream. Sweet-scented leaves and rhizomes are sometimes used in folk medicine or for food flavoring.

SITING AND CARE: Grow in any boggy or wet soil, in full sun to partial shade. Clumps expand slowly, but cut back occasionally to manage spread.

RECOMMENDED VARIETIES: 'Ogon' has narrow, 10-inch, golden-yellow leaves. 'Pusillus' is a dwarf, 3 to 5 inches high, spreads slowly; use between stepping-stones or around bonsai.

Marsh marigold's 1-inch yellow flowers bloom in spring above mounded clumps of shiny leaves.

CALTHA PALUSTRIS

KAL-tha pa-LUS-tris

Marsh marigold

- 2' by 2'
- Deciduous
- Grow in full sun at water's edge
- Lush, glossy green leaves 2" to 6" wide
- Zones 4–10

One of the most popular pond marginals, marsh marigold is a native to North America. Its bright golden spring flowers bloom above heart-shaped, shiny, dark green leaves for a month or more. Plants rise about 1 foot above the water and spread about a foot across.

USES: Marsh marigolds are a good choice to plant in damp spots near a stream, and they grow well in bog gardens. Grow them near other marginals to ensure that the bare spots they leave when dormant are hidden by their neighbors' foliage. Good with Japanese iris and moisture-loving ferns.

SITING AND CARE: Plant marsh marigolds in full sun so their crown is no deeper than 2 inches below the surface of the water. Plants are dormant by midsummer. Propagate by dividing plants or by sowing seed in boggy soil.

RECOMMENDED VARIETIES: A double-flowered form is available.

Crowns of needle-like foliage top erect stems of dwarf papyrus.

CYPERUS PROFILER

sigh-PEER-us PRO-fy-lur

Dwarf papyrus

- 1½' by 2'
- Deciduous
- Grasslike sedges
- Zones 9–10

Native to Africa, cyprus is highly regarded for its striking form, silhouette, and shadow pattern. It is an excellent water plant in frost-free regions, but a dangerous invasive in Florida.

USES: Grow at the edges of pools, in bog gardens, or in large containers. Where it's not hardy, plant in pots and take indoors for winter, or grow it as a houseplant. Attractive in dried arrangements.

SITING AND CARE: Sink in pots in the water garden. Grow in moist soil in full sun to partial shade. Remove dead stems in fall. In tropical and subtropical regions, grow outdoors in all seasons.

RELATED SPECIES: Umbrella plant (*C. alternifolius*), grows 6 to 10 feet tall; it has naturalized in parts of Hawaii. Note: *Cyperus profiler* is also sold as *C. isocladus* and *C. papyrus* 'Nanus'.

IRIS ENSATA

EYE-ris en-SA-tuh

Japanese iris

- 3' to 5' by 12"
- Deciduous
- Tall, swordlike leaves
- Orchidlike flowers
- Zones 4–9

Cool blues, purples, pinks, and white flowers bloom on sturdy stems 3 to 4 feet tall in dry soils, up to 6 feet in boggy soils.
USES: Excellent eyecatcher for boggy soils. Combine with queen-of-the-prairie (*Filipendula rubra*).

SITING AND CARE: Plant in full sun to partial shade. Provide rich, acid soil and plenty of water when in bloom. Space plants 18 to 24 inches apart.
RECOMMENDED VARIETIES: 'Cry of Rejoice' has deep purple flowers with yellow centers. 'White Heron' bears large, pure white flowers up to 11 inches across. Yellow flag iris, *I. pseudacorus*, thrives in standing water or very moist soil, Zones 2 to 9. Note: *Iris ensata* is also sold as *I. kaempferi*.

Japanese iris flowers, up to 8 inches in diameter, bloom in summer atop erect stems.

NELUMBO NUCIFERA

knee-LUM-bo new-SIF-er-a

Sacred lotus

- 3' to 7' by 2'
- Deciduous
- Leaves 1 to 2 feet in diameter
- Zones 4–11

These are large plants for large ponds. Peonylike pink or white flowers, about 6 inches wide and fragrant, sometimes double, come on tall stalks in summer.
USES: Common and highly regarded throughout tropical and subtropical regions of the world in large pools or ponds or at their margins. Flat-topped seedpods are dried and popular in exotic arrangements.
SITING AND CARE: Potential for invasiveness makes submerged containers preferable where planting must be held in check. Plants need several continuous weeks of sunny weather with temperatures above 80° F to produce flowers. In cold winter areas make sure containers of lotus rhizomes are below the ice line. Plants are hardy wherever submerged rhizomes don't freeze. Alternatively, gradually lower the water level, remove containers, and overwinter the rhizomes in a basement or garage.
RECOMMENDED VARIETIES: Miniature varieties—bowl lotus— are becoming popular. They have flower stalks that grow just 1 to 3 feet above the water surface.

Lotus need full sun six hours a day to maintain vigor and produce their exquisite flowers.

NYMPHAEA HYBRIDS

NIMF-ee-a

Water lily

- 3" to 12" by 3' to 4'
- Deciduous and evergreen
- Round, padlike leaves
- Flowers of hardy water lilies in white, yellow, pink, or red
- Tropical water lily flowers are blue, purple, and blue-green
- Zones 3–11

Hardy water lilies grow and flower readily in most regions and are easiest for beginners to grow. Tropical water lilies do not tolerate frost, require warmer temperatures, and begin flowering later in summer, although flower longer into the fall. Hardy water lilies can survive winter as long as the rhizome remains below the ice level. Flowers are somewhat less showy. Tropical day-blooming water lilies include blue-colored flowers. Their flowers come on stems several inches above the water level. Tropical night-blooming water lily flowers open only in early evening.
USES: Use in ponds or water gardens of any size.
SITING AND CARE: Plant a 6-inch rhizome section in spring by placing on soil in the pool bottom. Adjust height so that it is 8 to 12 inches below water level.

RELATED VARIETIES: Dwarf or miniature water lilies spread to only 1 to 2 feet wide.

Tropical water lilies begin blooming in summer; each blossom can last up to five days.

PRUNING AND MAINTENANCE

Meticulous gardening is a tradition in Japan, where there is no shortage of specialized labor. Here, gardeners prune and train a specimen conifer to maintain health while emphasizing the trunk, bark, and overall shape.

With some variation, the most basic horticultural techniques are universal. Using the same materials and tools that you would use in any garden, you can plant, feed, water, prune, weed, and clean your Japanese garden.

A Japanese garden, by its very nature, demands meticulous care. Weeds, pests, and diseases don't distinguish a Japanese-style garden from any other, so use the same control methods that you would use in any garden. The basics of horticulture need no explanation here. However, there are a few principles and special techniques that are unique to Japanese gardens that you should understand, especially for pruning (here the term includes pinching, shearing, and clipping) but also for other methods of shaping and controlling trees, shrubs, and perennials.

Some Japanese gardening techniques, such as wrapping tender plants for winter protection, are mostly picturesque. Often these techniques require hard-to-find materials, are not practical in the context of a residential North American garden, and so are omitted here.

PRUNING

Two very important, closely related, and often overlapping purposes of pruning are to control growth and shape the plant. A third reason to prune is to admit light to the lower branches and plantings under the tree or shrub.

For all three purposes, the season for pruning is important. Prune or pinch evergreens in late spring and again at the end of summer. Deciduous trees may be pinched or clipped in any season, but actual pruning (that is, the cutting of branches) is best done in late winter, before growth resumes in spring. Pruning to remove diseased parts of any plant should be done immediately when the problem is discovered, in any season. Fruit trees in Japanese gardens are pruned according to the universal calendar for the care of fruit trees.

All forms of pruning should be restrained when trees and shrubs grow under very stressful conditions, such as in salty or polluted air or in very poor or shallow soil. Too little foliage might remain to produce food for the plants.

PRUNING TO CONTROL HEIGHT:

A Japanese garden maker designs a garden with an appropriate ultimate size in mind for every tree, hedge, and shrub. Many gardeners, however, tend to let shrubs and trees grow indefinitely, without any regard for what would be considered too large.

The Japanese make gardens in which trees and large shrubs provide just the right degree of enclosure and just the right mass. These are determined according to the nature of each tree or shrub and its relation to the house, to another garden feature (such as a stone with which it forms a composition), or to the rest of the garden—in each case, a matter of proportion. In small gardens, it is particularly important to keep every plant strictly within the limits of its appropriate ultimate size. Most basic design principles depend at least in part on the size of the plants with which you are working.

It is sensible to use a slow-growing species whose size can usually be controlled by pruning. But even a well-chosen plant may eventually insist on growing out of bounds. If proper scale can no longer be maintained by pruning, the plant should be replaced.

To prune a pine tree, use by-pass pruners with scissorlike blades, which cut without crushing stems. Control the size and shape of pine trees by cutting a portion of the new growth, or candles, in late spring before they fully expand.

PRUNING AND MAINTENANCE
continued

Poles and ropes were once employed only to support branches in snow. Now they are used to train branch patterns.

Flexible wire wrapped around the branches, without catching foliage, is used to train individual branches.

PRUNING TO SHAPE: In pruning a plant to shape it, you essentially accentuate or exaggerate its natural form. Even topiary domes or mounds are shaped out of shrubs that are naturally of a rounded or mounding habit. Sometimes their shapes echo or blend with the shapes of nearby stones. A pine is often shaped to a layered, opened-up, spreading exaggeration of its natural shape.

Occasionally a shrub or tree is pruned without regard for its natural form, toward soft- or hard-edged angles. Such abstraction of form may balance the wild forms of adjacent stones and vegetation or create a transition between the symmetry of the house and the asymmetry of the garden.

Pruning a dense shrub or tree to shape may actually constitute shearing, if the foliage is very fine and the desired effect is smoothness. If the foliage is coarse enough to look butchered when sheared, or if a slightly more natural look is desired, cutting the individual tips will produce the desired form, but the plant will have a looser, less-controlled look.

Most trees and large shrubs, under ordinary conditions, grow more or less straight up. In Japanese gardens, differences in habit are valued, so that some trees and shrubs grow upward, but others are pruned to grow in curves or at slight angles. If the garden setting suggests a windswept mountain or a seaside promontory, all trees may be shaped so that they bend in the same direction. In any case, bending adds grace and a feeling of great age to the plantings.

PRUNING TO OPEN UP: Pruning to alter shape or control growth may also be a way to open up the plant. For example, a basic pruning practice is to remove vertical growth from an essentially layered form such as that of a pine. The shaping and limiting in height also allow light to pass through to the lower branches. The Japanese prune extensively to admit light and air to the lower branches and inner areas of trees and the plants growing beneath them. Healthier, less disease-prone plants will result from this practice. The lower branches remain alive, so that the desired shape of the tree is maintained. This kind of pruning must be done consistently to maintain the effect.

Generally, the method is to thin branches, first by removing any whose direction of growth is at odds with the desired shape, then by removing those that crowd, cross, or directly overshadow other branches. The remaining branches are staggered vertically.

Some species with naturally tiered branches, such as yew pine (*Podocarpus macrophyllus*), are pruned to remove foliage and branchlets from the center of the tree and from between the tiers to open the tree both laterally and vertically. The purpose of this style of pruning is aesthetic as well as practical: It shapes as well as opens.

A rope attached to the tree trunk and branch of a pine coax the branch downward.

In the traditional Japanese manner, a bamboo support bolsters a heavy tree branch.

A cement weight attached to an apple tree branch pulls the branch into a horizontal position.

Pines may be kept open, and their growth controlled by bud pinching. In spring, about two-thirds of each new bud is pinched off. At the end of summer, the needles on last year's growth are removed, along with some needles from the new growth. Also, if three buds formed where the bud was pinched, the middle one is pinched off. This pinching process is invaluable, but though it makes the tree airier, is not practical for most home gardeners because it is so time-consuming.

OTHER SHAPING METHODS: Pruning is not the only way to shape trees. By tying weights near the ends of supple (not brittle) branches, you can train them to arch. Branches may also be pulled down with rope (rather than wire, which cuts into and will damage the branch) and held down to stakes in the ground. When the arch is clearly permanent, the weights or ropes are removed.

When long, arching branches become too heavy with age and are liable to be broken by snow and ice, or by wind, the Japanese bolster them in various ways. A common method is the use of a T-shape support. For a more natural appearance, the wood of the support should be weathered; stained or weathered rope may be used as reinforcement.

Vines, particularly heavy, woody ones such as wisteria, also need a sturdy framework for support. Heavy bamboo looks appropriate, but heavy-duty commercial trellises will do as well. Be cautious about using climbing vines, such as hydrangea, on wooden surfaces such as the exterior of a house. Other vines can be attached to walls, arbors, fences, and buildings in the same way they are attached in occidental gardens.

PLANT REPLACEMENT

In Japan a standard form of garden maintenance is plant replacement. Sick, dying, malformed, or irremediably overgrown plants are removed and replaced by new ones. Because the plan of a Japanese garden calls for a given scale, as discussed early in this chapter, any plant that cannot be kept to scale through pruning is replaced. So is any plant that is past its prime. The Japanese garden exists to embody nature in an ideal state, and anything detracting from that ideal is altered.

This practice might at first seem drastic. Besides, many gardeners pride themselves on their success in keeping an aging plant going, or reviving an ailing one. But a Japanese garden isn't a laboratory. The Japanese value the preservation of the original garden design and the healthy freshness of the garden above any attachment to a plant, even an old tree, if it is declining or can no longer be kept pruned to the proper scale.

BONSAI

Meticulously trained and cared for, these plants have been dwarfed and trained to represent trees in their natural environment.

Bonsai require skill, patience, and years to create. These bonsai yews were carefully pruned to imitate the shape of full-size trees.

Bonsai, the artfully dwarfed and shaped container plants created by the Japanese and so widely admired in the United States, are not a traditional component of the garden. The Japanese grow them in a special area outdoors, apart from the garden proper. From time to time, as a prized bonsai comes into leaf, bloom, fruit, or fall color, it is moved into a living area—but only into a cool room and only for a few hours at a time. Some Japanese do display bonsai in the garden, along with other container plants that are there either temporarily or permanently.

If you use bonsai in the garden, be extremely careful that you protect these works of art that have taken much skill and many years to create. Generally, give them growing conditions appropriate to the same species growing in the ground. For example, keep a rain-forest plant in partial shade but a Mediterranean plant in a brighter, drier

The cascading form of this Japanese maple bonsai results from training the main branch to bend downward, extending lower than the container. The tree is displayed unobstructed on an elevated pedestal. Golden leaves will shortly fall as the tree becomes dormant.

Bonsai plants can remain in the same container for many years if you prune their roots every two or three years. In late winter or early spring, lift the plant and use sharp pruners to remove about a third of the outer roots.

Use a soft brush, such as this one made of hemp fiber, to sweep leaves and debris from the surface of the soil without causing damage to surface roots.

location. But always bear in mind how quickly the moisture in tiny pots can dissipate to the point that even the most heat and drought tolerant plant will die. Most bonsai prefer dappled shade, even those plants that might naturally prefer full sun. Higher than typical humidity is generally beneficial too.

When you move a bonsai plant into a new location, carefully observe it in the first two weeks. If the locations is less than beneficial, you'll see signs of stress, such as wilting or dried leaves. If this occurs, move the plant to a milder location.

Finally, be mindful that a miniature plant, certainly a contained one, may destroy the very effect in the courtyard garden that is most desired. Use bonsai in a staged display area of tables or benches to add the final touch to a Japanese-inspired garden.

Train branches of bonsai trees by wrapping wire along a branch and gently bending it in the desired direction. After several months, when the branch conforms to its new position, remove the wire. While in place, check frequently to ensure the wire does not cut into the bark.

RESOURCES

ASSOCIATIONS

The International Association of Japanese Gardens is one of the best places to start your own personal journey of discovery of this art form.

International Association of
   Japanese Gardens, Inc.
121 SW Salmon Street, Suite #1100
Portland, OR 97204
(503) 471-1386
www.japanese-gardens-assoc.org

MAIL-ORDER PLANTS

You can find many plants for a Japanese garden at your local nursery. Often how the plant is used and trained is more important than the specific plant. But the following nurseries specialize in Japanese garden plants.

Arborvillage
Box 227
Holt, MO 64048
(816) 264-3911

Asiatica Nursery
Box 270
Lewisberry, PA 17339
(717) 938-8677
www.asiaticanursery.com

Camellia Forest Nursery
9701 Carrie Rd.
Chapel Hill, NC 27516
(919) 968-0504
www.camforest.com

Collector's Nursery
16804 NE 102nd Ave.
Battle Ground, WA 98604
(360) 574-3832
www.collectorsnursery.com

Digging Dog Nursery
PO Box 471
Albion, CA 95410
(707) 937-1130
www.diggingdog.com

Eco-Gardens
PO Box 1227
Decatur, GA 30031
(404) 294-6468

Ensata Gardens
9823 E. Michigan Ave.
Galesburg, MI 49053
(269) 665-7500
www.ensata.com

Fairweather Gardens
Box 330
Greenwich, NJ 08323
(856) 451-6261
www.fairweathergardens.com

Fantastic Plants
5865 Steeplechase Dr.
Bartlett, TN 38134
(901) 438-1912
www.fantasticplants.com

Forestfarm
990 Tetherow Rd.
Williams, OR 97544
(541) 846-7269
www.forestfarm.com

Greer Gardens
1280 Goodpasture Island Rd.
Eugene, OR 97401
(541) 686-8266
www.greergardens.com

Heronswood Nursery
7530 NE 288th St.
Kingston, WA 98346
(360) 297-4172
www.heronswood.com

Las Pilitas Nursery
3232 Las Pilitas Rd.
Santa Margarita, CA 93453
(805) 438-5992
www.laspilitas.com

Matsu Momiji Nursery
7520 Troy Stone Dr.
Fuquay Varina, NC 27526
(919) 552-2592
www.matsumomiji.com

Miniature Plant Kingdom
13404 Harrison Grade Place
Sebastopol, CA 95472
(707) 874-2233
www.miniplantkingdom.com

Mountain Maples
Box 1329
Laytonville, CA 95454
(888) 707-6522
www.mountainmaples.com

Niche Gardens
1111 Dawson Rd.
Chapel Hill, NC 27516
(919) 967-0078
www.nichegardens.com

Plant Delights Nursery, Inc.
9241 Sauls Rd.
Raleigh, NC 27603
(919) 772-4794
www.plantdelights.com

Prairie Moon Nursery
Route 3, Box 1633
Winona, MN 55987
(507) 452-1362
www.prairiemoonnursery.com

Prairie Nursery
Box 306
Westfield, WI 53964
(800) 476-9453
www.prairienursery.com

Roslyn Nursery
211 Burrs Lane
Dix Hills, NY 11746
(631) 643-9347
www.roslynnursery.com

PUBLIC JAPANESE GARDENS

Here is more specific visiting information about the Japanese gardens mentioned in this book. Of course there are outstanding Japanese gardens in most every state and province in North America. For a more complete listing, see the Japanese garden database at www.jgarden.org.

Bloedel Reserve, Bainbridge Island
7571 NE Dolphin Dr.
Bainbridge Island , WA 98110
(206) 842-7631
www.bloedelreserve.org

UCLA Hannah Carter Japanese
   Garden
10619 Bellagio Rd.
Los Angeles, CA 90077
(310) 825-4574
www.japanesegarden.ucla.edu

Japanese Garden of Seattle,
   Washington Park Arboretum
1075 Lake Washington Blvd. East
Seattle, Washington 98109
(206) 684-4725
www.ciseattle.wa.us/parks/parkspace
s/Gardens.htm

Hakone Gardens
21000 Big Basin Way
Box 2324
Saratoga, CA 95070
(408) 741-4994
www.hakone.com

The Huntington Library,
   Art Collections, and
   Botanical Gardens
1151 Oxford Rd.
San Marino, CA 91108
(626) 405-2100
www.huntington.org

WATER GARDEN SUPPLIES

Of the many excellent supliers of
water gardening supplies, here is a
selection to get you started.

Lilypons Water Gardens
6800 Lilypons Rd.
PO Box 10
Buckeystown, MD 21717-0010
(800) 999-5459
www.lilypons.com

Paradise Water Gardens
Route 18
Whitman, MA 02382
(800) 955-0161
www.paradisewatergardens.com

Reeds 'n Weeds/Water Ponds
215 Normandy Court
Nicholasville, KY 40356
(859) 887-5721/(888) 909-5721
www.waterponds.com

Slocum Water Gardens
1101 Cypress Garden Blvd.
Winter Haven, FL 33884
(863-293-7151
www.slocumwatergardens.com

The Water Garden, LLC
5212 Austin Road
Chattanooga.TN 37343
(423) 870-2838
http://watergarden.com

Van Ness Water Gardens
2460 North Euclid Ave.
Upland, CA 91784
(800) 205-2425
www.vnwg.com

BAMBOO NURSERIES

These nurseries sell living bamboo
plants, and all are good sources of
information about bamboo hardiness
and culture. Some also offer bamboo
art pieces and implements (Burt
Associates), bamboo poles (Bamboo
Sourcery), and a variety of bamboo
structures for garden use (Bamboo
Giant Nursery).

Bamboo Giant Nursery
5601 Freedom Blvd.
Aptos, CA 95003
 (831) 687-0100
www.bamboogiant.com

Bamboo Plantation
642 Columbine LN SW
Brookhaven, MS 39601
(601) 695-1818
www.bambooplantation.com

Bamboo Sourcery
Sebastopol, CA 95472
(707) 823-5866
www.bamboosource@earthlink.net

Bamboo Texas
18022 Brooknoll
Houston, TX 77084
http://bambootexas.com

Burt Associates Bamboo
Box 719
Westford, MA 01886.
(978) 692-3240
www.bamboos.com

Burton's Bamboo Garden
Morrow, OH
(513) 899-3446
www.burtonsbamboogarden.com

jmbamboo
4176 Humber Rd.
Dora, AL 35062
jmbamboo.com

Lewis Bamboo Groves
265 Creekview Rd.
Oakman, AL 35579
(205) 686-5728
www.lewisbamboo.com

New England Bamboo Company
5 Granite Street
Rockport, MA 01996
(978) 546-3581
www.newengbamboo.com

Qvindembo Bamboo
Box 44556
Kawaihae, HI 96743
www.bamboonursery.com

Tradewinds Bamboo Nursery
28446 Hunter Creek Loop
Gold Beach, OR 97444
(541) 247-0835
www.bamboodirect.com

STONE LANTERNS, WATER BASINS, AND GARDEN ACCENTS

Most of the following specialize in
stone products, but one, Cherry
Blossom Gardens, sells many other
Japanese-related items including
complete bamboo gates.

Cherry Blossom Gardens
16159 320th St.
New Prague, MN 56071
(877) 226-4387
www.cherryblossomgardens.com

Mt.Fuji Stone Lanterns
14904 Smokey Point Blvd.
Marysville, WA 98271
(360) 651-2144
www.mtfuji.net

Nautilus Imports & Exports
122 Longleat Dr.
North Wales, PA 19454
(215) 412-7895
www.nautilusimports.com

Noble House and Garden
6408 Lakeside Dr.
Flower Mound, Texas 75022-5834
(888) 430-4455
www.noblehouseandgarden.com

Stone Forest
Box 2840
Santa Fe
New Mexico, 87504
(505) 986-8883
www.stoneforest.com

USDA Plant Hardiness Zone Map

This map of climate zones helps you select plants for your garden that will survive a typical winter in your region. The United States Department of Agriculture (USDA) developed the map, basing the zones on the lowest recorded temperatures across North America. Zone 1 is the coldest area and Zone 11 is the warmest.

Plants are classified by the coldest temperature and zone they can endure. For example, plants hardy to Zone 6 survive where winter temperatures drop to –10° F. Those hardy to Zone 8 die long before it's that cold. These plants may grow in colder regions but must be replaced each year. Plants rated for a range of hardiness zones can usually survive winter in the coldest region as well as tolerate the summer heat of the warmest one.

To find your hardiness zone, note the approximate location of your community on the map, then match the color band marking that area to the key.

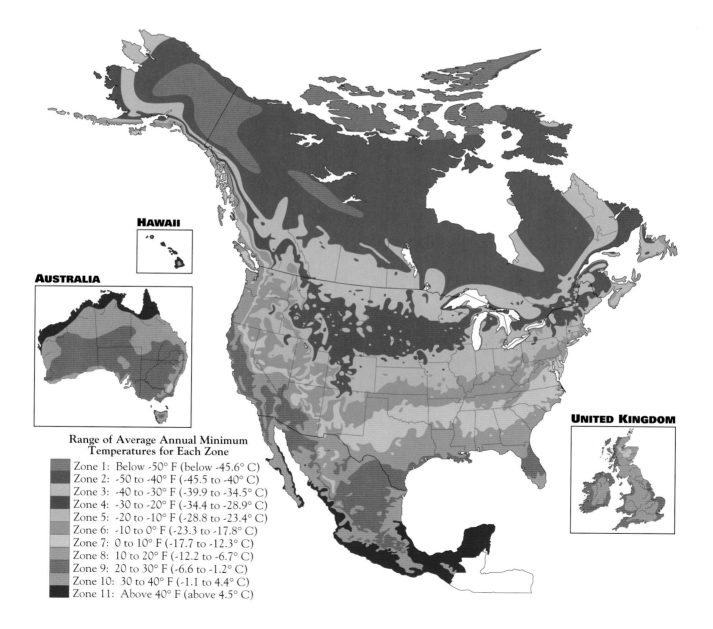

HAWAII

AUSTRALIA

UNITED KINGDOM

Range of Average Annual Minimum Temperatures for Each Zone

Zone 1: Below -50° F (below -45.6° C)
Zone 2: -50 to -40° F (-45.5 to -40° C)
Zone 3: -40 to -30° F (-39.9 to -34.5° C)
Zone 4: -30 to -20° F (-34.4 to -28.9° C)
Zone 5: -20 to -10° F (-28.8 to -23.4° C)
Zone 6: -10 to 0° F (-23.3 to -17.8° C)
Zone 7: 0 to 10° F (-17.7 to -12.3° C)
Zone 8: 10 to 20° F (-12.2 to -6.7° C)
Zone 9: 20 to 30° F (-6.6 to -1.2° C)
Zone 10: 30 to 40° F (-1.1 to 4.4° C)
Zone 11: Above 40° F (above 4.5° C)

INDEX

Page numbers in bold type indicate gallery entries. Page numbers in italic type indicate photographs and illustrations.

METRIC CONVERSIONS

U.S. Units to Metric Equivalents			Metric Units to U.S. Equivalents		
To Convert From	Multiply By	To Get	To Convert From	Multiply By	To Get
Inches	25.4	Millimeters	Millimeters	0.0394	Inches
Inches	2.54	Centimeters	Centimeters	0.3937	Inches
Feet	30.48	Centimeters	Centimeters	0.0328	Feet
Feet	0.3048	Meters	Meters	3.2808	Feet
Yards	0.9144	Meters	Meters	1.0936	Yards
Square inches	6.4516	Square centimeters	Square centimeters	0.1550	Square inches
Square feet	0.0929	Square meters	Square meters	10.764	Square feet
Square yards	0.8361	Square meters	Square meters	1.1960	Square yards
Acres	0.4047	Hectares	Hectares	2.4711	Acres
Cubic inches	16.387	Cubic centimeters	Cubic centimeters	0.0610	Cubic inches
Cubic feet	0.0283	Cubic meters	Cubic meters	35.315	Cubic feet
Cubic feet	28.316	Liters	Liters	0.0353	Cubic feet
Cubic yards	0.7646	Cubic meters	Cubic meters	1.308	Cubic yards
Cubic yards	764.55	Liters	Liters	0.0013	Cubic yards

To convert from degrees Fahrenheit (F) to degrees Celsius (C), first subtract 32, then multiply by $\frac{5}{9}$.

To convert from degrees Celsius to degrees Fahrenheit, multiply by $\frac{9}{5}$, then add 32.